Match of Minds: Electronic Affair

Willow Oakes

Trafford rev. 02/04/2014

 www.trafford.com

North America & international
toll-free: 1 888 232 4444 (USA & Canada)
fax: 812 355 4082

*D*edicated with love to my children and
their families who are learning and living
the benefits and the dangers of electronic
communications within this generation.

Acknowledgements

I read somewhere that a book does not get written without the help of others. I also believe that to be true. With much gratitude, I wish to honor the people who participated with bringing the story together.

Thank you:

- To the stranger who set the game.

- To the co-worker who was an active part of the story and advised research.

- To the proof-reader and editor who challenged the contents and presented ideas.

- To the friend who read it, gave her opinion and recommended caution.

- To the client who examined the story, validated the subject matter and offered suggestions.

- To the antique dealer who helped me to gain the chess board that was used as the book icon.

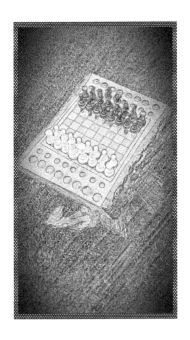

Match of Minds:
Electronic Affair

~ Each strategic play will equate
to a victorious conquest. ~

Contents

~ Prologue ~

You might ask me why I have written this book. It all began innocently when I opened my social media message box and found electronic mail from six different strangers. My social website is listed as private, and like many of my friends who have received these kinds of e-mails, my media status says I am single, which I believe is why I was targeted.

After disposing of five e-mails, I decided to click on one of the intruders' love letters and follow it. I found the escapade to be easily amusing, whereas I myself am a hopeless romantic. I would like to believe in the good of everything and everyone but I do realize if something sounds too good to be true then it probably is bogus. This episode has been my first experience regarding what I would consider to be a scam or catfish bait incident.

During this journey, while enjoying the playfulness, I continued my exploration to find out more about the person (or people) who were behind this electronic communication. In reality, even though I take pleasure in a good challenge, I found it very difficult to be the actress, the advocate, the investigator, and the author.

Because I have always enjoyed playing games that require strategy, I chose the game of chess to represent the playing field whereas each piece is designed to make specific moves according to their ability. The purpose of the game is to conquer your opponent's king that ends the game with a checkmate. During the sequence of the story I often challenged a game of digital chess on my electronic notebook for playtime. It was easy to incorporate this into the storyboard because the strategy of both was the conquest.

Throughout my research, I have gained a great amount of knowledge regarding the lack of safety when using electronic devices of today. Like many people, I would find it difficult to be without them for everyday usage. I believe this scenario is a rapidly growing scam tactic with potential danger where many people could become victims. It is because of this I feel it necessary to share my experience.

Those who know me say that when life deals me lemons I make lemonade and share it with many. I would agree with this and say, "I hope a lot of people will enjoy the lemonade."

~ ©Willow Oakes ~

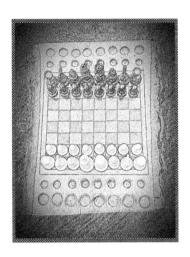

The Chess Board

Match of Minds:
Electronic Affair

Totti Rich Mac & Salina Toya

T his is a time when many people use electronic devices and the internet to keep up a correspondence. This way of communication produces instant gratification but does not always present good results. Realism and idealism frequently collide often causing potential danger for the people involved.

While many people want to gain or seek better than they have in their lives or relationships they expose their vulnerabilities with their actions, allowing a situation or circumstance to result in negative or dangerous reactions.

How does anyone steer clear of this? How does anyone avoid a scam or catfish scenario?

Enter the story to see what happens to Salina Toya and Totti Rich Mac.

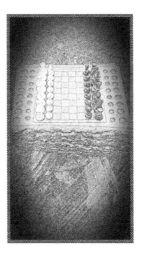

The Playing Field

Match of Minds:
Electronic Affair

Totti Rich Mac & Salina Toya

~ Introduction ~

~ The Meeting: Two Strangers Worlds Apart ~

S alina Toya and Totti Mac are in the middle years of life. Both are single according to their websites. They appear to be intelligent and very digital-savvy with electronic communications. These two strangers develop a friendship that begins with an online chat and continues with many emails. Will they connect by phone or meet in person?

Salina returns to her home after working a long day at her salon. She feeds the cat and dog, pours a glass of wine for herself then curls up on the couch with her tablet to play a game of electronic chess and to check her email. Salina finds a few mysterious letters in her other message box on her social media website. She is curious enough to open one even though she does not recognize the name Totti Rich Mac. Salina is surprised when she opens it because a chat box opens.

Totti:
"Hello Beauty. How are you?"

Salina:
"Hi Totti. How are you? Do I know you?"

Totti:
"I'm fine, thank you Salina. I don't think we know each other but I would like to know more about you. You look like someone I knew in the past."

Salina:
"Have we met before? I live on the northeast coast. You do not look familiar to me. My social media website is private. How did you find me?"

Totti:
"I'm new to this website. ☺ I just joined a few days ago. I've never been to the east coast but I would love to visit sometime. Did anybody tell you that you are one of the most beautiful women in the singles? I'll bet if they elected Miss single 2013 on this website, she has to be you! Your smile lights up my whole heart when I look at your picture and when I go through your profile. It must have been raining when you were born because I believe that God may have been crying for losing his most beautiful angel."

Salina:
"Awwww. Thank you. My parents were of Italian, Indian and Irish descent so I can thank them for the exterior but more so for the interior being. ☺ Many people have said I have an outgoing personality with transparency because I wear my heart and soul on my sleeve. Lol."

Totti:
"I guess we have one thing in common right now. Lol. My dad was from Italy, while my mom is a full country woman."

Salina:
"Alrighty then, hmmmm. Common denominators are good. Lol."

Totti:
"What are you doing right now? Tell me more about yourself? Maybe we have another thing in common?"

Salina:
"I am sitting here with my tablet checking my emails and playing a game of online chess. I love to play electronic chess because it is challenging and takes my mind off everything. I'm sorry; I don't think I know you. Can I ask if Totti Mac is really your name?"

Totti:
"Yes. My name is Totti Mac. My middle name is Rich."

Salina:
"Why is your profile empty? I do not see any family or friends?"

Totti:
"Like I told you I'm new here. Lol."

Salina:
"If you go to my website, you will learn a little about my character. Do you write, sing, or do arts in any category?"

Totti:
"You can ask me anything. I will answer you with an open heart."

Salina:
"Where are you from? What is your career?"

Totti:
"I can be a writer but singing isn't my thing. ☺ I'm a civil engineer."

Salina
"Great and you work for what company?"

Totti:
"I am self-employed. I am a global contractor. I do basically rig constructions and renovations or over water bridges and buildings. I have worked at many countries across the globe."

Salina:
"Impressive you must know many people. It sounds like you have traveled? Hmmm. I also have always been self-employed for years."

Totti:
"I am a widower. I lost my wife a long time ago."

Salina:
"I am sorry for your loss. Do you have children?"

Totti:
"I have the grace to work close with people. Children? Yes. I have one wonderful son who is such an adoring boy. He is kind and understanding. He will be 12 years old this August."

Salina:
"Ahhh, I sense your son will be your reflective spirit. A great gift of life! Totti, I think you also may wear your heart on your sleeve. Lol. Be careful on this website. Lol. They say it can be a very dangerous place. ☺"

Totti:
"I'm very careful. Thank you. You seem to know little about me now. Can you tell me more about yourself if you don't mind?"

Salina:
"I have two children who are grown, college educated and live close to me." ☺

Totti:
"Are you married, because you profile says your single?"

Salina:
"I have a successful salon business and have traveled to International Expos when available. I also have an Associate's Degree in Graphic Communications."

Totti:
"Oh, great. I guess your hard working woman!"

Salina:
"I am divorced of many years. I worked hard to raise two children. One family lives near me here on the mountain. I am hard working, yes. I keep a balance of work hard: play hard. Lol. Now, can you tell me more about yourself?"

Totti:
"My father died a long time ago. I also had my share of the pie when I lost my wife and best friend to cancer about ten years ago. Since then, my boy has always stayed with my mother in Spain. Since my wife died I have delved myself into work pretending to be hardworking even though I know in my heart that I was trying to just forget my pain and loss. Though it sky rocketed my success, am I really successful without a woman to crown me? I know I would give all I have to have the one thing money can not buy: a lifetime partner."

Salina:
"I am a simple, country girl who has been blessed."

Totti:
"I also work hard and I want to learn the habit of playing harder. Lol. ☺"

Salina:
"Sometimes my friend, one has to reach deep inside the soul to reiterate one's blessings and wholesomeness. One's completeness is defined as a matter of opinion."

Totti:
"I like traveling to new destinations always trying something different. Whether I'm experiencing an exotic spa in the Caribbean or eating at a new trendy restaurant."

Salina:
"Knowing in life your perimeter and what you will command not demand from another. At that point, another soul will align. ☺ Yes, myself also. I have traveled to many places."

Totti:
"As I could remember, as a kid I was a very cute one. ☺ Lol. One whom many bullies would target, but only to realize there

is a tough side to me. I could make a sober person dance. I could affect one with my smile. I grew up having older friends. Many would confide in me. To tell you the truth, I am a type that doesn't judge. I believe that no matter how dirty you may be, just come clean to me, and I will give you support."

Salina:
"I am easy going and have a lot of energy. I like the challenge of many different adventures. I get thrills from four wheeling. I have enjoyed trips with all terrain vehicles 4x4 riding in the canyons, adventure on the sand dunes, and wheeling on many other terrains. I also enjoy kayaking the rivers and lakes. I enjoy playing games like cribbage and chess because they are challenging. Chess is a game of strategy where each piece is assigned to specific moves. The challenge in the game is to conquer the other player's most important piece. Do you play?"

Totti:
"I do not play very well. It is a complicated game and I like to keep things simple. Lol. My usual line that I am known for is that life is simple for those who take it simple. I am very outgoing which helps greatly in my profession and I travel much but not all the time for my job. I like the outdoors just as much as I like hanging indoors. I just want to have a good time without expectations and would love to find a caring partner forever."

Salina:
"I love to take the train to the big city for a dinner theatre or Broadway show and maybe take the plane to venture the casino strip. I just enjoy new adventures of any kind. Yes Totti, we do appear to have many similarities."

Totti:
"I consider myself low maintenance and prefer jeans just with a t-shirt to dressing up, but if the occasion calls for it, I can look smoking hot. ☺Lol."

Salina:
"Like I said, we are alike in many ways only we are worlds apart. Where did you say you are from?"

Totti:
"Yes, but distance isn't a problem is it?"

Salina:
"This is crazy, huh? Sometimes distance makes for a good friendship with sharing daily events without impositions. Lol. Tell me Totti, do you like animals? Do you have any pets?"

Totti:
"Yes. I love all animals and yes I have pets."

Salina:
"Can I ask how old are you?"

Totti:
"I am 49 years old. And you?"

Salina:
"Older than you, but very young hearted with energy abound! Lol."

Totti:
"Oh, great, age is just a number that counts and not a big deal. The more we live the wiser we become. Salina, I'd like to know more about you, your interests, your likes and dislikes and what not. Will you tell me more about the place you live?

What does your busy time usually consist of? As for the distance, does that really matter for now?"

Salina:
"Silly. I am an old soul with a little girl's heart. I am a Christian soul, spiritual being who works like a woman and plays like a little girl. I will let you be my friend on this website then you can see my world. Do you have an email address?"

Totti:
"Thank you. Yes, I do have an email address."

The Pawn

Chapter ~ 1 ~

~ The Discovery: Two Lives To Learn ~

Salina allows her new friend Totti to befriend her on a well known social media website. She is curious about why he wants to be her friend even though he explains he is drawn to her beautiful smile, outgoing personality and appearance. Salina embraces Totti's compliments while she questions his purpose. She is amused and allows herself to be engulfed by the playfulness of his endeavor.

Totti:
"I am glad that I could get your attention Salina. You have a special thing in your heart, and I intend to find out what it is. It could take a lifetime to figure out but I really don't mind. Lol. You can write me sometime if you don't mind. It is TottiRichMac2@fakeweb.com"

Salina:
"Great! My email is SalinaToya2@realweb.com
Your middle name is Rich?"

Totti:
"Yes, it is Rich. I just sent you a friend request on reality chat."

Salina:
"OK, we'll talk on reality chat. Good night Totti. Chat soon."
☺

Totti:
"Sleep tight my new found friend Salina."

Salina:
"You do the same Totti." ☺

As Salina says goodnight to Totti, she checks the time and realizes she and her new friend were chatting for almost three hours. Salina is feeling excited and can't wait to share the story of her new connection tomorrow with her co-worker Kasey. She knows Friday is a busy day at the salon and she won't have much time for personal conversation unless she and Kasey have the same lunch break.

Salina has a lot of responsibilities because she is single, maintains a home and a successful business. She is apprehensive but so excited to have this new electronic connection that she does not sleep well and morning appears too soon. When the alarm sounds, Salina scurries around doing her morning routine as she prepares for another busy Friday at the salon.

When Salina arrives at the salon her first client is already waiting therefore Totti is tucked into the back of her mind so work can be a priority.

"Good morning everyone," Salina sings in her typical way. The day becomes busier than usual so that Salina and Kasey have light conversations in passing but are not able to have a lunch time together. As the work day nears an end Salina lets Kasey know she has a new acquaintance. Both girls giggle about the possibility of someone in Salina's life because she has been single and self-sufficient for a long time. "You never know what can happen," Kasey chirps to Salina as she says goodbye. "Have a nice weekend."

"You too Kasey," Salina says as she closes the salon, gets into her vehicle and drives home. Once home, Salina settles in for a quiet Friday evening because she is too tired to go out with her friends. After dinner she turns on her tablet to play a game of electronic chess and gets a chat pop up from Totti.

Totti:
"Hello Salina." ☺

Salina:
"Hi Totti, I got your email and I returned one. ☺ I also got a friend request on reality chat from a Billy Rock? I'm confused, why the alias?"

Totti:
"Some of my friends believe I look like Bill Rich. Lol. So sometimes I would call myself Billy Rock. ☺ I miss chatting with you and I hope you've had a wonderful day and didn't work too hard. I sent you a long email. You can read it and reply to me?"

Salina:
"So my new friend, how are you this evening? Yes, hmmm, Bill Rich. Lol. It appears to me: your intelligence far exceeds your rebel shield and is complimentary to your exterior being with a secure smile. ☺ I think I will enjoy our new online friendship with savoring conversations. I'll chat anytime. Lol."

Totti:
"Thank you Salina. Like me, I believe you work hard and always do your best. What you plant now, you will harvest later. I am fine and I hope you are as well. My week has been going smooth. With thoughts of you now in it, makes it more wonderful." ***winks***

Salina:
"So my friend, I did not realize this website displayed single people? How did you notice me and why? I am not on any singles networks. Years ago, I was on a common one and I learned that world appeared to be questionable as to truth or dare. Lol. ☺ I think many people on electronic dating sites are part of the instant gratification and disposability world. If they can click you on then they can click you off. Ha-ha! Don't you think? Anyway, truth be known, why me? What is it that appeals to you about me? Are you realistic or idealistic? These are all questions for thought, Lol."

Totti:
"Wow Salina that is a lot of questions! Lol. The key is to keep company only with people, who are like you, uplift you, and whose presence calls forth your best. I feel you are one of those people. ☺ I can tell you have a lot of energy. Lol. You have a beautiful smile too."

Salina:
"Ok, I have babbled enough. I'm tired. It is time for the water to hit my body and the pillow to catch my head. Lol. Good night Totti."

Totti:
"Good night Salina. I'll write an email. We'll chat again soon. ☺"

Salina logs off from chat, closes her game of chess, and fixes a hot cup of tea before getting ready for bed. She is content to be able to stay at home and use her tablet as a modern way to socialize, especially when she has to work a half day on Saturday at the salon. Salina always counts her blessings before closing her eyes for tranquil sleep at the end of her day.

Saturday morning brings sunshine and the birds singing tunes to another beautiful summer day. Salina awakens with new energy and prepares for her responsibilities as a home owner and business owner. Her ride to work is consumed with everything she has to do today because Kasey has the day off.

The day is extremely busy as most Saturdays are in a salon. After the last client leaves, Salina tries to write Totti an email but loses it. Before Salina realizes, the work day is done and she is cleaning and closing the salon. She hurries to get home before her friends arrive for dinner. Campfire and cookout are on this evening's agenda. Great company, good food and laughter are always relief from the day's tasks.

Salina and her friends take pleasure reminiscing about fun times while enjoying dinner by the campfire. When the evening is over and everyone has left, Salina cleans up then settles in on the sofa to check her email. She composes one to Totti:

"Hello my long distance friend Totti. ☺ It is now Saturday night at 10:00 pm eastern standard time and I am thinking it is about 6:00 your time? Before I closed my business today, I wrote a long email to you but it is not in my sent box so I am disheartened that cyberspace ate it. Lol. It may have been sent to archive. I will look when I return to work on Monday to see if it is there. My long hours are needed due to self sufficiency. ☺ I often go play on weekends but some times my Saturday evening is doing my friends' hair and ordering dinner to the business. I live my career and so many of my clients are my friends that I go out with. ☺ Some weekends, like this weekend, I just sit by the campfire at home with friends, eat, drink and share stories or play cards. Other weekends I go across the way for entertainment at the theatre. There they have comedians, jugglers, and other performances. The Theatre is on this website. Check their page out. They are my country neighbors. What does your weekends usually consist of? I look forward to you writing and sharing these things with me."

As Salina hits send, she notices there is an email from Totti already in her mailbox. She smiles as she opens it and reads:

"My dear Salina: It is now Saturday evening. It is again dark outside and I am sitting in my room in front of the monitor with the keyboard in front of me. Again I am waiting to see your name on the screen and have a nice chat with so many feelings in each word. I feel you are so near and so distant in the same moment. Every day I find something new in you, something that makes me feel different. I am sure of one thing, you are not only my friend, and you are something more, something deeper. Do you feel the same? I am not sure of your feelings. I'm not sure of what I am to you in fact? Am I just another name in your list or I am something special as you are for me? I am trying to find the answers by myself, but as I am trying I am getting scared of the answers that I might find behind all of this. I am scared and confused at the same time. Salina, after all of these days and nights I know that I found a friend, but I am not sure if it is the real friend. I know that I have found my first true friendship and I will keep it that way. I also know that I will give you all the care you need, or at least all the love you want me to give you. I know that I will care in a way I can not show and can not explain to you. I just want to be loved by you, at least as a friend. Believe me: I don't know why I chose you from this website. I didn't know you where single until I went though your profile. It's hard to believe a beautiful woman like you is still single. Lucky I am to have found you. I have a lot to offer to a woman who will love me for who I really am. I am a pretty good cook, so I know there are some key steps to producing any great dish. For instance, if you want to make a great stew, the first few things you put in the pot will determine the flavor, the texture and the overall greatness of the stew. The first thing I would like to put into our pot is a little compassion sautéed with understanding, sprinkled with loving care, and topped off with a nice piece of smoked tenderness. Let that simmer, cooking time varies and then add in everything else. Then savor the creation of our love."

Salina is too exhausted to return another email to Totti at this time. She needs to ponder this last one and write to him when she is not so tired. "Wow, that is pretty deep considering we don't really know each other," she mumbles. Salina shuts off her electronic notebook, closes her game of digital chess and decides she will drop Totti an email tomorrow.

The Rook

Chapter ~ 2 ~

~ The Questions: Caution With Words ~

After quite a few emails and chats with Totti, Salina begins to feel insecure because she believes it is too soon for deep emotional discussions. She asks Totti many questions about his background because of inconsistencies in much of his conversations. Totti always reassures her with his loving behavior and his so-called honor of this new friendship. He lets her know that wants to go further with this new relationship. At this point, Salina follows her instincts and becomes a little more cautious.

It is a gorgeous Sunday morning here in the northeast with golden sun rays spreading across the mountains. Salina stumbles out of bed, opens the curtains and mumbles, "Wouldn't it be nice to have just one morning to sleep late and lounge around the house instead of jumping out of bed to the loud sound of an alarm clock?" She hurries to get dressed and dashes out the door so she won't be late for church service. Sundays are very busy for Salina because she lives alone and after church she has to do the household chores inside and outside, go to the dump, and go to town to get groceries. Salina decides to take a late lunch break and check her email. She is still hesitant about her new friend and needs to tell him how she is feeling so she writes to him:

"Hello Totti, I must admit, I am amazed at your conversations and why a man like you is single. Myself? Hmmm. I live in a very realistic, not idealistic world. My journeys, good, bad or indifferent, have been many. I am a cautious woman with maturity whereas my youth I thought I was invincible. So, Saudi Arabia is a red flag in our conversation whereas there appear to be a lot scam emails? Correct me if I am wrong? Did you receive my email from yesterday? How is it a man like you is not out playing the field in your own backyard? Your story appears to be like two other emails that I denied through this website so I am now concerned. And in answer to your questions of my feelings toward you, I think it is too early in our connection to declare deep emotions. And no, I do not have a number of guys in line. I am looking for a solid, proven soul friendship before I would consider taking anything to the next level. Life's relationships develop by the moments in time collected. The hurry to seek a destination never grows strong enough roots to secure any partnership. So, what is it in truth that you my friend are seeking? Do you know what it is you want? It is now 2:15 pm here on the eastern coast and cloudy with showers upon us. I need to go mow the lawn before the rain, so I will check in later to chat. I hope you are enjoying your Sunday my friend."

Salina hits the send button then logs off from her mail and goes outside to mow the lawn before it rains. It takes her a while because her yard is big and has uneven ground. Just as she finishes and puts the lawn mower in the garage the downpour begins. She dashes through the rain to get indoors before the thunder and lightening begins. Once inside she cooks dinner, feeds the cat and dog and settles in for a relaxing evening.

Feeling content, Salina curls up on the couch with her notebook to check her email and sees she has one from Totti. She opens it and reads, "Hello my dearest Salina. Yes, one thing that I enjoyed today is reading your blissful mails. Thank you. Well, I guess we don't need to rush into anything serious right now. I believe our friendship will turn into something serious, but only time will tell. I can't stop looking at your pictures. I want to tell you that you're such a beautiful lady. Like I told you I am new to internet sense but I have a good feelings that this could be a chance for me to find a good woman to love and share great moments with her. I hope you are not working too hard at home today. Have a wonderful evening. I hope to hear back from you soon."

After Salina reads the email from Totti she notices there is another one so she clicks on it. Totti writes, "Salina, from the very first moment I saw you I knew that we were destined to be together. It has been a long time since a woman has captured my attention so fully. Your smile lights up my entire spirit. ☺ I have no doubt you are the woman heaven has made especially for me. Lol. Thank you for the comfortable conversations. No matter how slowly or at what distance our friendship develops, each day that passes makes our friendship grow stronger. Although I know it's hard for us to be apart, I know there is nothing that can keep us apart forever. Our desires will continue to stretch across any distance, over every mountain and ocean between us. Nothing can stand between us, and nothing will stop me from meeting you! I am here with open arms. I hope you have a great Sunday. Did you attend church service? I am looking forward to your sweet email soon."

"Wow," Salina whispers to herself, "this is crazy. How can this be real?" She is very confused about the whole thing. Even though the electronic connection appears to be phony, Salina is enjoying the association. She has not told anyone about Totti but Kasey because there is a part of her does not think it is genuine. "It's all harmless and nobody's getting hurt," she murmurs. "It passes time and I can be a hopeless romantic without any expectations," she giggles. With that in mind, Salina shuts everything off and goes to bed ready for a good nights' sleep.

It is still raining in the morning when Salina awakes. There is no need to hurry today because Monday is her day off from the salon schedule, so she decides to lounge around the house in her pajamas. With coffee in hand she checks her smart phone to see if Totti wrote another letter. She gets excited to see one from him so she quickly opens it and it says, "Good morning my wonderful Salina how was your night? Did you ever think of me out of the blues? Lol. I awoke to another tune of life. You know I am always smiling ☺ but I discovered my heart just had a true smile for the first time in these few days since I started writing you. So will you tell me the truth? Are you the angel? Did God hear my cry and decided to send one of his best angels to come be my guardian? Whatever it is, I don't want to stop feeling this way. Charisma once said, "When it rains, look for the rainbow". So when life gives me this kind of opportunity I seek the climax, really. I think the reason I have been able to open up in speech and expression with you is not just unusual, but before, the beating of my heart pounded like a drumbeat and was lost. I have been looking for a rhythm like you. So the compliments are what bring the best out of me. Lol. ☺ My present and last contract is on the Abu Dhabi platform and it is located offshore United Arab Emirates. I still have few more weeks here before coming back to States. Sorry I didn't mention this to you before. And Salina, you will be the first person I want to see. I think you captured my interest just because you are being true to yourself. Well, that is something good because they say we attract love by the emotions we display. We retain love by the emotions we possess. And if I am able to finally be your true friend, it means unbreakable because that is one thing no one else can ever be. You! I fly on the usual way to the platform almost everyday with my men, and now everyone seem to know I am becoming happier because I glow more. Lol. ☺ Did I tell you my friend married last year someone he met on a dating website? Troy is one person you would surely love. He is a very close friend since college and has been with me all the way. And yes it is true, there are two things we can never escape in life, and we can never tell how, when or where it happens, and it is love and death! I pray to God that I may have found my chance and I will do everything to make the dream come true. I don't need anyone to take advantage of my weaknesses or my strengths. I need someone who will appreciate me for everything that I am. And if in this pure way you can feel sentiments for me, then it is a point to prove that. I hope you have a great day my dear and you write back to me soon. I always love hearing from you."

Salina is surprised at Totti's letter. She is feeling very inscure about this new friendship and hesitant to pursue it as a serious relationship. At this point, Salina feels like she needs to investigate Totti's background so she spends a little time researching. It appears he has a few profiles that are listed with similar names on a few different social media sites. "Hmmm, this is all very interesting. I wonder why he does not display friends or family on any of these pages," she mutters as though she were talking to someone else. She looks up at the clock to see what time it is and exclaims, "Gosh, I'd better get going if I am going to town to get salon supplies."

Salina scurries to the city to get her weekly work provisions then delivers them to the salon, grabs a bite to eat then returns home before dark. "Whew," she says, "what began as a lazy day turned into a whirlwind." She giggles as she settles in for the evening feeling as though she got a lot accomplished today. Suddenly she gets a social media text message on her smart phone and it is from Totti so she responds using electronic chat:

"Hello Totti, how are you today?"

"Hello beautiful,☺" says Totti.

Salina:
"Hey Totti, Thank you for you compliments. As one would say, you also are easy on the eyes."

Totti:
"Awwww, thank you beautiful. Are you busy right now?"

Salina:
"It is 7:13 pm here in the northeast and it is a beautiful summer evening. I am just making pasta with chili and enjoying a glass of wine. ☺ What time is it there? Where is there?"

Totti:
"It's after midnight over here in Dubai. It is 3:13am. I awoke and had to check to see if you dropped me an email. Lucky I found you on here."

Salina:
"Wow Totti, you're not asleep? Lol. It's 3:13 am there? Hmmmm."

Totti:
"Like I said, I just woke up to check my email."

Salina:
"Totti are you a night owl?"

Totti:
"Yeah, I don't believe in much sleep."

Salina:
"That is funny: I also do not require a lot of sleep, just good sleep." Lol.

Totti:
"Another thing we have in common. Lol."

Salina:
"So if there is a six hour difference in the time between us then when I am home and online 7 pm-10 pm, you are usually asleep? No wonder we don't catch each other. Lol."

Totti:
"Yeah, I had to stay up late to catch up with you on here. After reading your last mail to me on here I feel we need to chat."

Salina:
"Really? And?"

Totti:
"Salina, like I told you when we first met on here, I'm very new to this and I don't know how this works but I have a few friends that have met some good and nice woman online and they got married happily ever after. ☺"

Salina:
"It is ok my friend, but you do understand why I have to be cautious?"

Totti:
"Yes, I do understand."

Salina:
"Totti, I think you are an intelligent man with many wonderful traits and find it hard to believe you are also single?"

Totti:
"Well, I am so single! I know it's hard to believe but it is true."

Salina:
"Is there not a woman where you work, play or stay that would enjoy the opportunity to be your partner?"

Totti:
"Of course they are a lot of women out here and everywhere but one loyal friend is worth ten thousand relatives."

Salina:
"Without question, you are handsome, hard working, intelligent, sincere, and meeting many, so why haven't you chosen a steady partner????"

Totti:
"I want to be very close to someone that I can respect and admire and have somebody who feels the same way about me, but I haven't found one yet."

Salina:
"Did you not tell me that you have a son?"

Totti:
"Yes, I do have a young son."

Salina:
"Totti, did you receive the email I sent but thought cyberspace ate it? Do you see your son much? Where is he while you are so far away?"

Totti:
"Yes, I see him. He is very understanding and he has been telling me to find someone to love, but I refuse. People do tell me how I look but I see myself has a normal person with no different from others."

Salina:
"I guess that is another thing we have in common. Lol.
Did you say he lives with your 80 year old mom? Huh. Really?"

Totti:
"Yes. I wonder why you're still single. You are beautiful, hardworking, open minded and I am very sure you love deep. Salina, you do need a great man to complete you.☺"

Salina:
"My desires have always been to seek a soul who could walk with me, beside of me and not behind me or in front of me."

Totti:
"My desire is the passion for which I live my life.☺"

Salina:
"Amen, my friend, well said. I will reiterate that. ☺"

Totti:
"My desire will be fulfilled when I reach my destination, which is none other than a place in woman's heart."

Salina:
"So, just like me, the desire as the passion for which we live our lives may be not equivalent and unreachable to many who have crossed our paths. Don't you think?"

Totti:
"Do you believe in true love?"

Salina:
"Yes, but if it were so easy, you and I would not be single.☺"

Totti:
"Yes, not easy but I believe in true love because death can not stop true love, it can only delay it for a little while."

Salina:
"True love, hmmmm, I believe love has many facets."

Totti:
"I believe to love someone is to understand each other, to laugh together, to smile with your heart and to trust one another. One important thing is to let each other go if you can't do this.
God only knows the reason that we met here and share a smile."

Salina:
"I believe also in love as that way in a perfect world my friend. We both know a perfect world does not exist. Lol. I have the desire to love like that, but I believe it has to have time of nurture to grow."

Totti:
"I believe if you take away love, the earth would be a tomb."

Salina:
"Totti, you and I might be a reflection of persona that has been allowed to connect for self-assessment. The worlds apart allow reality so that we might both understand the next phase of our lives. Don't you think?"

Totti:
"Yes I do. So Salina, what do you really think about having someone in your life?"

Salina:
"The truth is that I find the little girl inside playfully dreams of the innocence of loving: then the woman in me fears the hurt of rejection. As a woman, I want to be in love and also love my best friend. People tell me my expectations are set too high and I make myself unobtainable, and you? What is your story?"

Totti:
"Like I said, you are a beautiful and a hardworking woman. I am very sure you're picky. As for me, people come into our lives and walk with us a mile, and then because of circumstance they only stay a while. They serve a need within the days that move so quickly by, and then are gone beyond our reach, we often wonder why. I believe in angels, the kind that heaven sends. I am surrounded by angels, but I call them my best friends."

Salina:
"Wow, you write like I do! Lol. Please check out my website. Be sure to go to the catalog of photo stories that is on the left side where my face is. I am sure you will enjoy them!"

Totti:
"I believe the mind is what should listen, but it is the heart that should speak. I believe those who wish to sing will always find a song."

Salina:
"Stop, alright, already! Are you for real? Lol. I feel like I am talking to myself. Ha-ha."

Totti:
"We really do have a lot of things in common."

Salina:
"I am a simple, barefoot country girl with a heart as big as the ocean and a soul as deep as the Grand Canyon. I have a mind as vast and infinite as space and I feel that I have already left a legacy as deep as the earth's core."

Totti:
"I really do understand you. Salina, I can help you write more poetry if you let me."

Salina:
"I believe maybe now, there is a time for myself to align with another person into the next phase of my life."
Totti:
"If you are willing to trust in a person when all others tell you to go against it, and if you are willing to risk getting your heart broken because you believe in that other person, then that is true friendship love."

Salina:
"But my dear friend, only when one is freed from yesterday can one today set forth a new journey into tomorrow.☺"

Totti:
"Yes, you are right. I also believe that."

Salina:
"Oops, set free. Lol. Sorry, tired, excuse the spelling. Lol."

Totti:
"Lol. I understand Salina. I'm sure you worked hard today as you must do everyday."

Salina:
"My dear friend, without expectations, I will cherish our new and unique electronic communication."

Totti:
"In my world, I walked to a different drum. You came along and joined me in my journey. I am now in harmony and at peace in the world of friendship. No one realizes the beauty of friendship, until you're caught in it. I'm thankful I met you Salina."

Salina:
"I think I am grateful we are miles apart so that we may continue to bond in soul in a world that is moving so fast people have forgotten what feelings are like. Don't you think?"

Totti:
"Yes, I think much more than we realize."

Salina:
"I believe that the electronic world has set new standards with robotic behavior that is becoming a component of instant gratification and disposability."

Totti:
"I think though miles may lie between us, we're never far apart, for friendship doesn't count the miles, it's measured by the heart."

Salina:
"Do you realize many people over 50 years of age do not have much digital comprehension therefore are a world away from understanding many things in today's generation? Therefore, I believe that the emotional element of many younger people might be disintegrating and becoming a non-reliable feed for the soul."

Totti:
"I also think that is true. Salina, it is 4:40 am here my friend and I should sleep now."

Salina:
"Oh, no! Go to sleep my friend. It is only 8:42 pm here in Northeast."

Totti:
"Let me get a few minutes sleep. I would like to read an email from you when I wake up."

Salina:
"Thank you for your sincerity.☺"

Totti:
"I am sincere Salina. Check your email because I sent you a long email yesterday. You can reply me back if you wish. I would like that."

Salina:
"Good night and sleep well my dear friend."

Totti:

"What you feel is what you are Salina and what you are to me, is beautiful. Have a great night my friend and I hope to dream about you. ☺"

Salina signs off from chat feeling pleased with her new friendship. Even though she is weary, her mind is racing as she wonders what it would be like to sit together with Totti and talk over a cup of coffee. "After all," she mumbles, "Isn't that the normal mode for people to get to know more about each other?" Salina has a hard time sleeping because of her mixed emotions and her excitement to share all of this with Kasey when she gets to work. The alarm sounds and Salina rises to a beautiful morning, fixes her coffee and is raring to go. She writes an email to Totti before she goes to work:

"Hi Totti, here in the northeast, it is Tuesday, the bright rays of the golden sun peeked brightly through the trees as its golden rays spread across the sky hued of ice blue. The music sung loudly by the bird's echoes in my ears as a smile crosses my face reflecting my thoughts of you. Good morning Totti my dear friend. I hope you slept well even though your night was short. As you read this email, I will be very busy at the business and it will be mid-day here in the Northeast. We had severe thunder showers throughout the night here so my driveway was challenged again. Yesterday I filled the sink hole with rocks and a bag of cement powder so I hope the sun dries and sets the culverts today. There is always something to repair when one lives in rural country area. What is like where you live? Are you city or country oriented? Preference? I posted a link about the state I live in on my web page. Check it out if you chance. It shows some of the Northeast destinations that many tourists travel here to see. Do you know anyone who has visited the northeast United States? I do understand that you are a long way from here. Lol. You mentioned your present and last contract in your work is located off the Abu Dhabi platform. What exactly do you do for work? Are you an engineer sub contractor? Civil Engineer where? You certainly are very digital savvy. ☺ I am impressed with your communicative skills. Well my friend afar, I wish you well wherever you are. ☺May your morning be good and your afternoon too. Wear a smile on your face and know I'm thinking of you."

She hits send, closes her electronic tablet and dashes out the door so she won't be late for work. When she arrives Kasey has the salon open but nobody is there yet. "Good morning Kasey," says Salina. "How are you? Did you have a nice weekend?"

Kasey smiles as she answers, "Yes I did, and you? Did you hear from your new friend Totti?"

Salina giggles, "Yes Kasey, we chatted for quite a long time. Who would have thought I could have these conversations with someone I've never met and yet feel like I want to keep because I'm enjoying his communications: Hmmm: it's strange, huh? What do you think about it all?"

"Well," Kasey replies, "Everything happens when it's supposed to even if we don't know why. Just go with it and see where it takes you. You deserve to be happy but be careful. Be sure to find out more about him and where he comes from."

"Thanks Kasey. I appreciate your opinion and your honesty. It will be interesting how this all plays out, huh?"

Kasey cautions, "Just make sure you research his name and follow his information."

"Yeah, I've looked him up and found his profile," says Salina. "There are so many questions that are unanswered. So much I want to know! He appears sincere. It makes for a heck of a story! Lol."

Salina and Kasey laugh as they go about their salon work for the day. The day proves to be busy and Kasey is saying goodbye to Salina at 5:00 pm.

There is never a dull moment when work involves the public. People come and people go making the work day pass quickly. Today ends very differently than usual when a stranger comes into the salon at closing time and takes the money bag that contains the work day income. It all happens so fast. Nobody's hurt and new security measures are learned. Safety is the lesson of the day. When the police arrive, Salina repeats her 911 call for the reports and then discusses the event feeling like this is an isolated incident. When all is said and done, she finally closes the salon and goes home.

As Salina makes the turn into her long dirt driveway, she feels relief when her motion light brightly welcomes her home. As she unlocks her door she whispers, "There's no place like home." She is feeling the aftershock of the robbery event, pours a drink and decides to take it easy tonight. Salina eats dinner, feeds her cat and dog then settles onto the couch to check her email hoping to find one from Totti. With anticipation she notices one and opens it:

"Good evening my awesome friend. How was your day? I trust you had a good day. I want to tell you that I am an oil platform supplier and major contractor. I work mainly with the government on their platforms by contract. I am a self-employed engineer. I live in small city where the platform is located. I don't know how to explain this, but I know if I don't get a message from you I will feel bad. I know I do think about you momentarily. I find myself smiling for no reason. At that moment I look in the direction where you are wondering if you can see the same sun, moon and stars as I do. Lol. Yesterday was a good day for me. We were on our usual cruise, me and the whole ten men crew: the Musketeers. Lol. ☺ Troy, Stefan, Ian, Mafoose, Walsh, Chan, Naky, Izaak, Zaid and I. Lol. There are many men of different nationalities. They are my men at work but we are more like friends than they are being my men. We have come a long way working together. These men are expert at work, very professional, but they play real hard too. One of them named Troy met and married a girl online. Shirley's parents couldn't let them go after the wedding in Marietta, GA. Oh Shirley is the woman married to Troy. Lol. I told them how I have become entrapped in a journey with a woman I just met online. And yeah now they have seen pictures and they still want to hear more over time about you. Now the funny thing about this is that the two mischiefs, Walsh and Naky actually bet who would be closest to you. They see me as not only an employer or friend but as a father figure too. I try to make sure my men are alright. I mean I would take a bullet for any of my men if necessary not only my musketeers but the other 30 men working on the oil platform too. They would love to be able to tell you. According to them this is one man who has waited ten years to have a good home and would be the best husband and father any day at anytime. I mean I will be a husband and father first before any other thing. This is how I weigh happiness: it is in the joy of my family not in gold or wealth. I am one who would never make you cry, for all my life I have giving nothing but joy to people around me. I have seen some pain in life. I have seen the goodness in people. I have been rescued by strangers, hurt by friends and I have seen that life is what we choose to make of it. I want to give all of myself to you. I can feel fear for being hurt, but that is normal to feel. Whereas I am a man of God I know fear is not of the lord so I will not give in to it. I can see this journey of ours is going well. Perhaps some forces making the journey smooth. Lol. I will sure follow my heart all the time and I am holding your heart strong and firmly. I am one who gives nothing or I give everything. Once you get me, you have all of me. Lol. I am a man who is known to have no fear, a high risk taker on business. But I also believe that everyday in our lives actually goes through risks. I have shown you all I am. I will never pretend to win your heart and I will never hide any part of me from you. I took my last contract which is the biggest peak of anyone in my field, it cost me all and even loans to finance since it is my duty to handle local expenses till the end of the job so we get paid fully. So if I did not take such risk how can I get high gain? Such is the life we live my dear. I know I can be comfortable looking at your eyes everyday of my life, what do we call that? Lol. I only want someone that I can't wait to get home to be with and someone who calls even when she is busy or tired. Someone to come into my arms that I can hold in my strong arms and whisper my wish to her ears as I look lovingly into her eyes. I have to go now my dear. Please write to me soon ok? I will be thinking of you. Your new friend, Totti"

Salina sits back after reading Totti's email and says out loud, "Who is this guy who tells me everything but tells me nothing at all?" Salina is feeling depressed and insecure as she responds to his email with many questions.

"Hello my long distance friend, how are you this evening? I hope everything is well in your world and your complicated contract is going well. Totti, can you please clarify a few things for me? I am quite confused with where your home is? It was my understanding that you live in California, USA and yet you speak of a home in a small city on the platform? I am sorry that I do not understand your world. Can you please explain more? Are you not an American citizen? Which government do you work with? What affiliation do you have, if any, with a company I mentioned that I discovered your profile is linked to?

"Oh my, maybe my confusion is also the results of a bad scenario that happened to me at my business tonight. L An unknown woman came into my business at closing time and robbed it then she left quickly, jumped in a car with out of state plates and sped away. It all happened so fast. No one was hurt and it appeared to be the actions of desperation. She only got $80.00 and change cash with ten checks written to the business, but I'm sure when she grabbed the money bag there was no thought of a small business usually deals with plastic or personal checks. There is an all points bulletin out for the couple. Today, the police will view the security cameras from the store across the street. What is this world coming to?

"In April of this year, while on my return trip from an annual Expo, I found myself in the middle of the city bombing lock down. L Situation and circumstance always appears when I am in the middle of an equation brought on by other scenarios, none of which are ever produced by my actions, but instead the recipient of someone else's bad action. L So you see my friend, I so do wish that I could trust all but by many lessons I have to always be reminded by elements like these, that in order to survive, my mind has to been keen and my awareness has to be sharp. L My dear Totti, my energy at this time is exhausted and my soul weary and yet I sit here very late at night in the northeast while I write to you this email. Time will tell my electronic friend.

"So, how are you? I hope you have had a good day. Did you receive my other email? I am still recovering from this experience. I just posted the robbery story on my web page. L Hopefully I will sleep tonight. I do enjoy our email adventure. I am feeling though like it would be nice to hear from you. ☺ Good night. Be well my friend."

Salina is feeling lonely after such an exhausting experience and wishes that some how, some way, sometime she and Totti could really hear each other's voice on the telephone. She sighs, "Maybe this would feel more real to me if we could talk." And on that note, Salina exits her email, closes her tablet and calls it a night. Morning always comes too early.

Salina feels better as she awakens to the singing of the birds outside her window with the sun peeking through her curtains. She rises and prepares for another work day. Her morning routine has become her coffee in one hand and electronic tablet in the other so that she can check her email. Once again, she opens one Totti has sent to her and it reads:

"Hello my wonderful friend. How are you this Thursday morning? Why am I getting addicted to my messages? Lol. I get a good glow on my face just waking up to read from you that's just wonderful. How was your day and night? I knew something was missing since I haven't smiled all morning till now. Lol. Maybe I could sense something good ahead of us. I'm doing fine now because I got your email. Thank you so much. I replied back when I saw your post about the robbery and I made a comment on your media page. L I am sorry. I missed chatting with you and I hope your day is going well so far. Don't work to hard because someone out here is thinking about you. Thoughts of you warm my heart. You complete me and I went to bed last night with a vision of you next to me. I slept like a baby all night, because I was not feeling alone. When I awoke this morning to see if it was real or if it was a dream, reality hit me that it was only a dream. Lol. Every step I make I feel safe, because I feel your presence around me. ☺ "Thank you for all the beautiful emails you have sent to me to my friend. I know that neither one of us had in mind that we would meet someone on the internet and be friends but it has happened. And for that, I have no regrets. In fact, it is one of the best things that have ever happened to me in years. So, more about me: I have a 3 bedroom house and it is kind of a pretty good house. It is kind of quiet and peaceful to live there in California. That's my house while I am not on any of the oil platforms. The home I'm staying in right now is just for work. I rented it to stay near the platform. Let me tell you more about my background. My father was an international business man who met this Irish orphan whose only family was close friends. Mom said there was something about the man that no woman could ever resist. Sometimes she says she sees same in me. Lol. During my father's global movement and while I was twelve years old, I left to study in Lethridge Alberta in Canada where I got the first degree in Civil Engineering. I later moved on to join him back in the state. My father died when I was a young man. I met my wife and best friend in Paris. She was a fashion model. She had a very good at heart. Actually I could say I met her in a funny way, I would explain that later. She is late now. She passed away few years ago. Do you know that many ladies always start off by asking where Mr. Right is? Lol. Then I think to myself, whatever happened to Mr. Left? Describing me in such a limited amount of words would not be enough, but to sum it all up I can honestly say that I'm a down to earth person, open-minded to try new things. A relationship should be a 50-50 split without that possessive attitude. Beauty is in the eyes of the beholder, keeping in mind that beauty is only skin deep. I like traveling to new destinations and always trying something different, whether experiencing an exotic spa in the Caribbean or eating at a new trendy restaurant.

"My job: The present project is my last on the field and I shall quit field works and continue my works from my home office in California while my men do the field. I think I really have gotten to this height because I embraced work for so long trying to get over my wife that I worked this hard but I think I now realize I can move on.

"My dream: I have told you how my typical dream day would be like: I just want to spend the rest of my life enjoying the fruit of my labor. ☺ I just want a woman who would be my best friend and everything else. You know someone whom we would still love each other more as the days pass by even when we can't make love anymore and all we could do is play bingo. Lol. I just want to thank you for coming into my life. You took me by great surprise. I wouldn't ever think that I would be as lucky to have you as my friend but now that I have you I don't ever want to let go. I hope you write to me soon. Totti"

Salina looks at the clock and realizes she will be late for work if she doesn't get going so she shuts off her tablet and goes to work. When Salina gets to work Kasey greets her and asks her about Totti. Salina tells Kasey what Totti said about his background, his job and his dreams.

"Wow," says Kasey, "that is quite a bit of personal information, huh?"

Salina answers, "Yeah. It all appears real but then again it doesn't. It is so different than anything I've encountered before. What do you think Kasey?"

"Well, I think you should just go with it and see what happens," Kasey playfully replies.

"I know, right? I've got nothing to lose," Salina giggles, "I'll check later to see if he's written again."

The day gets really busy for both girls and before they realize it another work day is done. It is time to close the salon and go home.

When Salina gets home she quickly checks her tablet to see if Totti wrote again. She gets excited when she notices two emails from him. She opens the first one and realizes as she reads it that Totti wrote it early this morning because it reads:

"My Loving Salina, I hope you had a splendid night because I sure did with your thought all over me. I am currently at work and can't get you off my mind so decided to drop you a note that you can read when you awake. I got your email and I am pleased to read from you. Your emails melt my heart a lot. I know there is an ocean between us. I wish that it weren't true, for every minute I think about you, I yearn to be with you. Though a lot of distance lies between us, you'll always be in my mind and my heart, I pray for the day we'll never be part. When I'm checking my email, I will be thinking about you. When I go to sleep in the loneliness of my room and give in to wonderful dreams I will definitely be thinking about you. I know someday we will meet and spend our lives with each other. I have waited for somcone like you, and now that I have found you I will never let you go. I believe that two people are connected at the heart, and it doesn't matter what you do, or who you are or where you live. There are no boundaries or barriers if two people are destined to be together. Much love to you my true friendship. ☺ Did you get my email questions? I anxiously await your response my dear."

"Whew! This is all getting deep," Salina says out loud. "Hmmm, I wonder what questions Totti means." She clicks on the other email and discovers there are the questions for her to answer. Curious, she scrolls down through and then pauses. Salina needs some time to digest these inquiries from Totti.

The Knight

Chapter ~ 3 ~

~ The Intimacy: Two Hearts To Hold ~

Salina and Totti appear to be getting closer as they share emotions and sentiments regarding their hearts and desires. Both are feeling comfortable as they seek questions and answers about simple everyday living. Salina begins to want to get closer to Totti but often detours him when he tries to encourage a bonding. The intimacy where two hearts begin to feel close now develops a shadow with a protective edge.

Salina pours herself a glass of wine and curls up on the couch to reread Totti's last email that says:

"Good evening my wonderful friend. It was a good day here. You actually refused to leave my mind and I did dream about you last night. Lol. What you have done with my heart, you have no idea. ☺ Now, when I am with the rascals, they don't really comprehend since I don't really need talking much again without saying anything. You actually make me want to sing now. ☺Lol. Ok, Salina, I have these questions for you so breathe deep inside and out and then answer after thoughts."

"Do you believe that magical love still exists even in these odd times we live in?

"If you were to choose between your family and all wealth in life, what would you choose?

"If I ever for any reason have tears in my eyes, what would you do?

"If I kiss your neck for so long in the middle of the night while you sleep, what would you do?

"If I brought you breakfast in bed will you pay with a kiss?

"Would you support me in all ways on my charity events?

"Would you rather buy a thousand dollar wrist watch than give a hundred to someone in need?

"Have you won the first and best victory which is over yourself?

"Do you love yourself enough to know why you deserve love from others?

"Do you agree that war is a good answer to any political dispute?

"Would you leave business environment with me from time to time so we can run away for vacation, just the two of us?

"Will you let me drop you off at work?

"Do you believe a man is truly in happiness without love?

"And now without fear, my last question, would you be with me today, tomorrow and forever?

"They say guys have to realize that they have to be sweet, caring, gentle, and honest and still have that sweet little thing about them that drives any girl crazy: and that's reaching her heart. No matter how much you try, if you don't reach her heart, it won't ever be worth-while. Well, with luck and chance, this medium did let me know your heart and reach it. ☺Lol. The only odds I see possible are if we ever lied to each other one way or both ways. L I know I will never do that in my life because I can never build a relationship on lies. I know for sure you can never lie to me then meeting will only be a compliment my dear. That is what I believe to be true. So anyway, while we were on the usual cruise on the boat but not working and since we work every single day dear, the musketeers did notice I was fantasizing about you so they sang their naughty song and put in your name and mine. Lol. Yeah, I really imagined you on the boat with me and your head on my chest. I am naughty, huh? Lol. I've got to go back to work. Be sure to take good care of yourself for me my sweet true friend, till I can come do it myself. Hehehe. I will be thinking of you all day my loving friend."

Salina feels like she is a teen who is blushing as she rereads then answers Totti's email.

"Whew, Totti, I think I need an ice bath. Wow! This whole thing is crazy! I was truly amazed as I read your story and answered your questions. And now it is your turn to breathe deep inside, think about the answers I have given to you and reciprocate, if you may."

1. "Do you believe that magical love still exists even in these odd times we live in?"
    "Yes, I believe that love is magical in the beginning and that the continuation of the magic can only be maintained if both people involved give the relationship 100% effort and live and love with appreciation of the gift."

2. "If you were to choose between your family and all wealth in life, what would you choose?"
    "In my lifetime, there has never been and there will never be any question of family priorities. Family reigns over anything monetary."

3. "If I ever for any reason have tears in my eyes, what would you do?"
    "If for any reason, you should have tears in your eyes, I will give you all of the compassion necessary to ease your pain and respect your wishes. I would embrace you with comfort."

4. "If I kiss your neck for so long in the middle of the night while you sleep, what would you do?"
    "Yah . . . kiss my neck for so long when I am asleep and . . . I won't be asleep no more . . . Lol."

5. "If I brought you breakfast in bed will you pay with a kiss?"

"My dear man, needless to say if you bring me breakfast in bed . . . hmmmm . . . pay might be play. Lol."

6. "Would you support me in all ways on my charity events?"
   "To support you with your charity events would be reflective upon my own life style whereas I have and always do live my life helping others."

7. "Would you rather buy a thousand dollar wrist watch than give a hundred to someone in need?"
   "Sorry, I am not nor have I ever been, a thousand dollar wrist watch girl. I have and always will reach out to those around me in need."

8. "Have you won the first and best victory which is over yourself?"
   "Unsure of the question you ask regarding victory over me, I will say this, I know who I am. From the many years that I have worn rose colored glasses and carried a band-aid box for the world, I now am able to define my life with the ability to command not demand what I will or will not allow near or into my perimeter."

9. "Do you love yourself enough to know why you deserve love from others?"
   "Again I say, I have had to learn what I will and will not tolerate from another person's behavior. Life is too short. To give love equates to receiving love."

10. "Do you agree that war is a good answer to any political dispute?"
    "First let us define political dispute. I see it as a battle in seeking power where lives should not be taken.

Nevertheless, the physical battle for empowerment has been all beings way since the beginning of time."

11. "Would you leave business environment with me from time to time so we can run away for vacation, just the two of us?"
"A good business environment is necessary to succeed and provide, however, equally important is the ability for one to be able to escape the responsibility of business. Any relationship can only survive if human priorities are maintained and over ride monetary desires. Escaping into playful modes most relationships will remain strong and healthy."

12. "Will you let me drop you off at work?"
"And why wouldn't I let you drop me off at work?"

13. "Do you believe a man is truly in happiness without love?"
"My dear man, happiness is an individual determination to be content and love is a multifaceted attachment that is received in many ways."

14. "And now without fear, my last question, would you be with me today, tomorrow and forever?"
"And without fear, my loving Totti, I will answer your last question. Yes, you have reached into my soul and captured my heart. The development of our electronic connection has rapidly grown into a true, deep friendship with both of us expressing the desire for more. If we both continue to live in the mode of gradually existing in each other's everyday life, you and I will secure our position into a concrete relationship today, tomorrow and forever. I believe if we choose to align at this intersection of our lives, we will successfully continue on in life side by side in

whatever level of a committed relationship we both decide.
The spiritual medium, as I believe in, was very right when she gave her advice to you. Amazing as it really is that even though the two of us live a world apart physically, we both have arrived at this intersection in our lives with what I believe is a spiritual guidance."

Salina is feeling very connected to Totti at this time. She feels excited because she just sent to him the answers to his inquiries. She is feeling pleased and yet confused with all of the ohs and what ifs of this electronic love affair. Salina wants to say so much more so she writes another email to Totti.

"Hello my dear Totti. How are you this evening? It is Friday night at 10:30 pm here in the northeast and I am still smiling over the email I sent to you earlier today. You asked then I answered. Please print the attachment, read and ponder. No need to be confused or fear any heartfelt emotion because we both have been spiritually connected and given the opportunity to travel a discovery journey with each other. ☺ I want to discover something else about you everyday and make the memories of sharing moments. There need be no explanation with our hearts awakening only the sentiments of caring and excitement of growing closer with the promise of truth.

"This connection that began as an electronic viewing from two people who were worlds apart has now become an everyday emotion within each soul and felt in each one's heart. The intensity of feelings from two people whose world have yet to be seen, appears to be challenging their hearts producing questions of what will be. The wish of these two souls is to wish each other well.

The desires of both, will they be met? Only time will tell.

Please be safe while you are in your world, my friend.

So my dear friend, wear your smile and sing to happiness so that your rascals enjoy your glow and marvel over your contented heart. I will sleep now with the same contented heart. ☺

Smiles to you my dear friend Totti."

Salina has so many feelings surfacing now with all of the intense conversations that are happening between herself and Totti. She is getting very addicted to the emotional feed and is scared that it will all disappear. Anxiety builds in Salina as it all appears to change during the week. Salina writes to Totti everyday and feels apprehension when she gets no reply. L

Day 1: "My dear Totti, it is Saturday night at 12:55 pm as I lay here awake thinking of you and wondering if you are well because I did not hear from you today. This evening my friends Stefan and Brianna brought dinner to cook over the open fire. We all enjoyed fresh corn cooked still in the husk over an open wood fire, steak on the grill and wine for spirits. Do you enjoy the campfire dining? While we chatted, I spoke of you and where you were working on the platform. They asked me if you were safe because of the tension happening overseas. Are you safe my dear friend? I hold you in my heart and I pray for your safety. It is my understanding the international waters are under travel warnings. How does the rising tension in that country affect you and your contract? Even though we are an ocean apart, my dear friend you are held in my heart. I hope you got my email. I look forward to hearing from you soon."

Day 2: "Good morning Totti, how are you today? It is now Sunday morning at 1:05 am and even though I am tired, I find myself wanting to write to you. Thank you for sharing your background and dreams. I will cherish the journey of our orientation with no expectation of destination. That my dear friend is the ingredients for true everlasting friendship and the core of any concrete relationship. As I read your family background, I realized your life's roads have been similar to your father's path. Do you believe you are a replica of your father? After all, wasn't he an international business man with a global movement? And yes, I understand your mother's statement that there was something about the man that no woman could resist. Hmmmm, I guess you are just like your father. ☺ Do you think your son will tell the same story someday? Will he be his father's replica, a handsome, compassionate, intelligent, loving man? I am sorry you have had the painful journey of inevitable destiny but you are so blessed to love that deep with your wife and your best friend. Please Totti, never feel like you can move on. Your wife is and always will be a part of you: as your son is a part of both of you. ☺ Who we all are today is the ingredients of where we have been yesterday which makes us all better for tomorrow. That is all truth and an element of acceptance. Thank you for asking to be my friend on this website. I am glad I did not pass up the opportunity to discover such an amazing, wonderful person! Beauty is only skin deep, because a beautiful interior can make a plain exterior absolutely gorgeous!"

Day 3: "Hi Totti, It is now Monday night at 10:09 pm. I have had a busy weekend, and you? I hope you had a good one too. Can you please tell me the time whenever you write emails? I do not quite get the time change. Is the time 16 hours different here to there? So today I bought a new truck, a four wheel drive loaded. Nice ride. I have my other one sold, makes it easy to register and insure. Living on the mountain, I need 4x4 for winter. What do you drive? What is the climate like where you are? Hope you are well. I'm thinking of you."

Salina is caught up in the romance and the emotional feed of her electronic affair. She is feeling now like something is wrong because Totti has not written since he sent the inquiries to her last Wednesday. There are times when Salina feels that Totti is still a little reluctant to provide any real personal information about his life. She doesn't know if she should be concerned with Totti's lack of communication and she is beginning to wonder if he is in danger. "How can I be this worried about someone I barely know? Oh, this is crazy! There is just so much that I do not know about this man," Salina mutters to herself. She decides to write to him again because she can not get to sleep with all the questions going through her mind.

Day 4: "Hello Totti It is now 11:00 pm Tuesday and I can't stop thinking about you. I wonder, did I say something wrong? Are you alright? Does our story abruptly end here? I have you in my prayers as I ask for your safety. I miss your emails. Even though we don't really know each other, I feel an absence without your connection. Be well my friend." L

Salina is disheartened with Totti and feels like she wants to research to find out more about him. "How can I let someone I know so little about affect me this way? It is so discouraging to have him tell me so much yet tell me nothing. L Oh, my! I am so confused with this electronic affair! I'm beat. I'm going to bed," she sighs and turns out the lights.

A few more days go by without any communication from Totti until suddenly Salina gets a text message from him that says, "Check your email sweetie." With anticipation, Salina checks her email on her smart phone and eagerly opens Totti's electronic letter:

"Hello my true friend. I am sorry for being absent. I am writing you this email to tell you how much you mean to me, and to thank you for coming into my life. You are something I never thought could exist for me. You are one of the best things that has happened in my life, and I don't regret being with you. At first I was confused. I didn't really know what I wanted. I didn't know if I would want to take a chance again and actually take you seriously. So, I decided to come close to you as a friend and find out who you truly are and what you are like. You appear cool, honest, and nice and we have quite a lot of things in common. You have traits that I really liked in a woman. So I have taken a chance and now I am with you. Well, a lot of time has passed and I have discovered new things and a new me. You have truly changed me. Still, in a way I am scared because I am actually growing a true feeling inside my heart which I just can't explain. I know it's there waiting for you to come and uncover it. I truly don't know what your feelings are but I don't want to force you in telling me what you don't feel towards me. I want to receive love and trust from you when you truly ready and mean it. All I ask from you is to show me you care and not hide anything, to also have trust in me the way I do in you. My heart has already found it's way you. I want you and no one else. You mean everything to me. I think we should try and make this work. You have to know you're the one and only one I want. Not only are you perfect for me, you're the perfect friend and I hope we can and will be more. I could never ask for better than what we have had. I am hoping you're feeling the same way because my heart is set on you and only you. They say opportunity only comes but once: but in love, a well deserved lover would always get a second chance and mine is here. Lol. I will never let go of you. You have won all that is me. I mean after the magical love I had, one would think such may never occur again. With faith in the lord and dedication to finding love, I ask God for a wife and he gives me an angel. He is always giving me the best. I am glad to know when you think of me you smile because the most wasted day is that in which we have not laughed. And laughter is the one true thing everyone will always need. Truly there is one moment in your life when you are with someone and you feel like the world has stopped and your life seems so perfect. Make sure you never lose that person. I will be glad that you accept me, for when you welcome love with your whole heart, soul and body, love will welcome you with all its sweetness. The path can never always be sweet but the things that people in love do to each other they remember and if they stay together it's not because they forget, it's because they forgive. In my thoughts of you there is an underlying love that is present in every word and every glimpse. I hope you feel it as I do, for it is what I am and ever I will be. Have you not noticed that being in love is what makes working all week bearable? It makes cruising with your windows rolled down feel like you're riding in a convertible. It makes you dance to the rhythm of the copy machine and makes every night really feel like the weekend. Lol! Sweetheart, I have just few weeks to hangover here, do you mind picking this naughty lover at the airport? Once I get the exit schedule, you will be the first to know. Let me know which airport is closest to you, but can I tell you a secret? I may be tempted to give you a first kiss at the airport hope you are not too shy, Lol. I can always be naughty right? I would love to get closer to you. How about reality chat? I just want all the mediums to be used so I can feel closer to the woman I have fallen in love with and that is you! Lol. Before I sleep and after I wake up and all the hours in between you occupy my mind now. ☺ So, practically every moment of the day you are in my thoughts. Salina, I miss you. Though miles may lie between us, we're never far apart, for relationship doesn't count the miles, it's measured by the heart. I will be thinking of you so much today. Please take good care of yourself for me until I can start doing that."☺

Salina is stunned with everything Totti has just told her. Feeling shocked as she gets the first email read, Salina finds another one in her social media message box from Totti. She opens it and is very surprised as she reads more of the same type of expressive contents. Salina is taken back a bit because Totti unexpectedly appears to be pouring out his heart to her. She is experiencing so many mixed emotions and feels her heart racing as she reads his letter:

"Hello Sweetie, I'm sorry for the late reply, been a little busy. How are you today? How is work at the business? I am going to put my feelings in words, on this page. Since the day I met you on this website, I haven't been the same. My feelings I just can't seem to tame. I am starting to care for you in a different way. I think of you every day! I love everything about you! Your smile, your eyes, your hair, your body, etc . . . I am pretty sure you got the point. I can't get you off my mind. Sweetie, you've got me feeling different. I know you may not feel the same, but my feelings just keep growing each and every day. Well, what I am trying to tell you is I am sprung and I am falling in love with you. Yes, this is true! But I understand if you don't feel the same. I know these sounds lame, but I have to let you know how I really feel. And this is no lie, I am for real. Sweetie, you've struck me as being mild mannered and quite lively. In fact, your elevated words added some spice to my life. To me, you're a rose that should be protected from thorns around lest they prick you. You're an angel that shouldn't be hurt. You're also honey that should be covered against contaminants. By the grace of God, I'm ready to do whatever it takes to make you happy, I promise. I love you so much, and can't wait to be with you. I want to give you my heart and soul. I don't care about anything else in the world because I am in love with you. I love you. Thank you Salina for you made all of my dreams come true. I could not ask for more. I am the luckiest man in the world to be called your Best friend, I'm truly honored. Thank you. How I wish words could express the thoughts that I have towards you. If I should say I love you then the greater percent of my words are still unexpressed. But of course, I must say my heart beats for you and my heart longs for you. Have a wonderful day. I can't wait to read from you soon."

Amazed at how Totti's attitude has changed, Salina writes back to Totti with more questions:

"Hello Totti, It has rained hard all day here at home. Check out the videos of my yard where the fish were knocking at my door. Lol. ☺ Tomorrow my driveway needs repair. Oh well, when you live in the country and are single there is always so much to do and so many repairs to maintain. So, how are things in your world? There are so many things I want to know about you. How is your job going? Do tell me more about yourself? What is your favorite color? Do you drink coffee? Do you play poker or Cribbage? What kind of music do you listen too? What do you like for aftershave or men's cologne? What is your favorite pastime? And your favorite food is what? What is your favorite season? Your zodiac sign is? Do you dance? What is your favorite song? I could go on and on but I will stop there and await your reply. Take care, be safe."

Salina is stunned when Totti doesn't waste time and answers her questions immediately:

"Hello Salina, I am most passionate about my relationships with my friends and family. I am also an avid sports enthusiast who enjoys attending local professional and collegiate games, as well as participating in a number of sports (skiing, tennis, swimming, etc.).

The three things which I am most thankful for are my relationships with family (that's just my mother): opportunities to experience different cultures through travels and good health. My friends describe me as: affectionate, loyal, outgoing, and genuine.

What is my favorite color?
My favorite color is red.

What is my favorite type of exercise?
I like to jog and to do press up for my body fitness so to be healthy. Three of my best life-skills are: *keeping physically fit, volunteering my time to causes I care about, and finding new adventures and unique experiences.*

The most important thing that I am looking for in a person is: *they must have adventure, sense of humor, enjoys travel, honest, loving, and to attend local sporting events, working out, spending time with some friends and family.*

The things that I can't live without are: *my morning email from you, my passport, watching the Sea Hawks, Grey's Anatomy, friends and family.*

Do you drink coffee?
Yes, I drink it black.

Do you play poker or cribbage?
I play both poker and cribbage.

What kind of music do you listen too?
I listen to blues, classic, and country and any kind of good music.

What do you like for aftershave or men's cologne?
1 Million For Men.

What is my favorite food?
I love good food but I have no favorite. Lol.

What season is your best?
My favorite season is summer.

Your zodiac sign is?
Virgo

Do you dance?
Yes. I do love to dance and I hope you're a good dancer.

What is my favorite song?
I love to listen to Memphis Minnie, Kissing in the Dark, Big Joe Williams, Baby Please Don't Go, Little Walter and My Babe.

"Salina sweetie, I miss you and I can't stop thinking about you. I look forward to your email. Please write soon. Totti"

Salina:

"Hi Totti, How are you today? What time is it where you are? It is Saturday afternoon here in the northeast. Maybe we could talk on the phone? Who is your cell phone carrier? I have a wireless network that can connect anywhere. So do tell: Virgo, hmm . . . Is there a birthday in the near future? Is this the big one? How will this affect you? This is often a transitional phase with many making life changes, and you? How will you celebrate? Your birthday is when? Do you think you have the Virgo traits? I'm just curious my friend. ☺ I am an Aries 100% Can you handle an Arian? Lol. I hope you are out enjoying your weekend my friend. I hope to hear from you soon my friend."

The Bishop

Chapter ~ 4 ~

~ The Challenge: Two Minds To Match ~

As their friendship develops, Salina and Totti both appear to be drawn in by the playfulness and challenge of the 'match of minds'. Salina is becoming amused by Totti's sudden emotional sentiments. Totti does not realize yet that there is nothing Salina enjoys any better than a challenging, competitive game where each move requires strategy like the game of chess.

Salina is enjoying her weekend by spending her time with her household chores and being outdoors working in her flower gardens. She takes a break to write to her long distance electronic friend:

"Hello my dear friend, how are you today? It is Sunday afternoon, the storm has passed here and all is normal. The day is beautiful and I am just enjoying being at home doing typical chores, cooking, cleaning, gardening, mowing, etc. The sky is blue, the air is clear, and temps are in the 70's. It's almost perfection, except the voided feeling of your companionship. As I sit here on the deck, I wonder how you are and what your world is like today. My mind is wandering as I question if you and I are real or a figment of my imagination. Other than my coworker Kasey, nobody knows we have been writing. I've never had a pen pal who was such a secret. Lol. Doesn't this all feel strange to you?

☺Maybe it is possible we could talk by phone? My number here in the states is +56723469601 carried by a wireless network. We have been writing through the summer and I feel it might be time to hear our voices over the phone. Don't you think? I hope to chat soon. I'm thinking about you and what your voice sounds like."☺

Totti responds:

"Hey Sunshine, I hope you are having a wonderful day with a lot of thoughts about us. I swear. I don't know what I would do without you! You mean more to me than I can say. I hope that our relationship lasts forever and ever! I would love more than to be your friend. I just know that I will always be by your side loving you and supporting you in whatever it is you want to do in life. I love you Salina! I can't just stop thinking about you. Lol. You must wonder why I call you sunshine. ☺I can't get the picture of you off my mind. I felt like giving a hug. Lol. Just as the sun, lights up the earth, you light up my life. The only one I have met, with a heart so bright. It just seems like yesterday, you came around my way. You changed my whole scene right away, with your outstanding smile and outward personality. The only reason this was possible is because you must have portrayed yourself well and you have been yourself. That is good, because if I ever fall in love with you for beauty, I wouldn't walk more than miles to see more beauty. If I love you for wealth, I wouldn't walk more miles to see more. If I love you for smiles, I would see more in television. Lol. But the only thing I can fall in love with you that can't be gotten by anyone else is being you! That is absolutely what no one can ever be! Like I said, it takes a life time to try knowing the reason why you feel the way you do with some people. The answers are never there. Trust me, the day relationships start falling is the day people can figure out the exact reason they have loved each other. Life is boring if perfect. Life is worse when there is nothing to change about anything. The balance in life is based on the facts that the medical practitioners would run out of business if we are all hale and hearty. The legal practitioners would die of boredom if there aren't offenders. If everyone is vegetarian, Oh my! Guess how many people would not earn a living. Christians bring out the best in Christianity because of the presence of Islam. If everyone is rich, wealth would be meaningless. Who would do the laundry? Who would drive the car? Who would guard who? Who would keep whose money? Lol. The essence for this short word is that, if you can read the meaning in this. You are my woman for sure. The moral of the speech is that, we were all created for each other. There is much fun in helping. We can all be better if we accept the fact that we can't live without each other. The world would be a better place if we can start accepting things we can't change. Because, the only constant thing in life is change! Sitting here thinking about you, brings out a part of me that loves everything. Lol. I have a proposal for you this wonderful day. Because I know you at least care about me, after all you wake up to check on my mail and know if I am still alive. Lol. That is something. So I want your help today.

There is this woman, whom I just met, and I could be scared about how she has gotten my attention so soon, but I would be stupid to submit to fears. I noticed that she already has a place that can not be replaced in my heart. Who could ever think of hurting such a woman who only wants happiness? I want you to help me find her and tell her that I am not known for fears. I know a journey of a thousand years start with a single step. A man who wants to fly must at least learn to stand on his feet! Tell her if she is willing, I would love to take her hands. I am a man who gives nothing or everything. Once I have her hand, I can promise her forever. Tell her I know this is not going to be a kid walk. Tell her I know there are times we would argue in future. But tell her I would teach her to know that even while we argue we would still be holding hands, because there are many sides to a coin. Tell her life is short but we can make paradise out of it. Tell her that her worries have become mine now because I do not really know how she has done it. Tell her that coming across her was by chance, communicating with her was by choice but then falling for her is beyond my control. You know where to find her my dear, just go to your dressing mirror and you would find her staring back at you. Lol. Please, look into her eyes and speak this to her for me.

"Salina, I want to tell you that you are the most beautiful person I know, inside and out. I see that more clearly with each passing day. I love everything about you, about us. You do something to me that no other has. You have made me so happy, and the happiest I've ever been. You give me the most amazing feelings inside, the feeling of being in love with you. I still don't know what I did to be so lucky to have you in my life. My dream has come true. I am so thankful that in this short time that we've been sending emails, we have grown so much. I can't wait to see what the future holds for us. I love you. Yes. You can call me if you'd like. My international business mobile is +609523709128 it is active no matter where I go. Please do say your name when calling so we don't mix business with personal. Lol. I must warn you that my accent is unsorted and I hope you like it. I have been told I speak in a sexy way. I guess it is the European in me. Lol. All I can say is you're the best surprise life has given me and your capacity for love, caring, and understanding never ceases to amaze me. I have truly been blessed by finding you and I will never let you go!"

Salina reads Totti's letter and responds with her usual sharing of events in her life:

"Hello my loving friend, how are you today? It is 4:12 pm on Monday here in the northeast and raining again. LI am a little discouraged because I dragged my dirt driveway yesterday for 2 hours to level all of the gravel from the washouts all summer. My driveway is 650 feet off the tarred road and is a lot of plowing and dragging gravel. Lol. OOps. I forget I am not typing on my tablet. Lol. This pc is different. Anyway, you are the only sunshine in my day today. ☺ I just sent you an email. My turn to get a little scared, but still be grateful for the caring I feel. Thank you my dearest friend. I am truly blessed and no matter where you are or will be, I am grateful to have you in my life as my friend. So, will you answer some more questions? Lol.

Do you play a strategic game of chess?

Do you enjoy picnics and walks in the woods?

Do you kayak?

Do you like hockey?

Do you like mudding and 4x4 adventures?

Do you like baseball?

Do you play pool or darts?

What is your favorite alcohol?

Do you smoke?

If you could only take one more trip anywhere in the world, where would it be and why?

Do you like animals?

Can you leave work alone when you go out to play?

Do you like to be spontaneous or does everything have to be planned?
Do you enjoy the snow?
Do you enjoy walking in the rain?
What time is it where you are now?

"I've got to go back to work. Lol. A client just came in. I will chat later. Before I go, here is some poetry for you to enjoy:

You and I live two worlds so far away, and yet we share heartfelt sentiments everyday.
How intellectual will either of us prove to be if we do not assess this reality?
It has been only two months since our first hello, now both of us feel as though we might be in love.
Everything appears that the spiritual union was joined from the angels above.
Could it be the spirits have bonded together each one of our souls, to love, honor and cherish into the years we grow old?
Reality needs to be a priority with what we both decide, and only time shared can display truth without any facts to hide.
There is no question both souls have lifetime connected, but the visible reality could still be rejected.
How either of us will react in the flesh, is yet to be seen.
The relationship already between us positions the essentials to fulfill a possible dream.
There is no doubt that passion and desire now rages in your heart and mine.
Days need not be hurried only developed and savored with time.
Let each one of us clearly understand, the gift of a loving friendship that has been awarded to this woman and man.
The power of the loyalty and dedication for this relationship to long term survive, will be determined as truth and without hurry for what could prove a very long ride.

*The compatibility we have might allow for a partnership the
rest of our life, whether it is a sincere friendship or husband
and wife.*
At this place and time only God and the spirits know.
What is in place for us and how our hearts will grow?

"Enjoy your day my dear Totti. Take care, wear a smile,
and know someone in the northeast absolutely enjoys who you
display!"

Salina is anxious to learn more about her dear friend who
is her own little secret that she hasn't shared with anyone but
her coworker Kasey. Kasey is also interested in the story of
this electronic affair and the true identity of Salina's new
friend. Salina and Kasey say goodbye and close the salon
for another work day. After enjoying the summer evening
outdoors, Salina goes indoors to write to Totti before she
retires for the night. She writes to him and shares her day:
"Hello Totti. How are you? It was a gorgeous day here in
the northeast. When I came home from work, I played outside
with my dog and my neighbor's dogs, and then I jumped in the
hammock for a rest. While I lay there watching the sunset, my
thoughts wandered to you and how your world was treating
you. Have you ever heard of geocaching adventures? Look
it up if you chance. Today, one of my clients was talking
about cache discoveries using longitude and latitude locations
all over the world. I thought of how I am on a rare cache
discovery across the ocean. Lol. Anyway, check it out if you
like adventures! My geocache name is registered as RU4RL.
You'd expect that of me, huh? ☺ Lol. So, I hope your absence
from our email connection does not mean you are not well? L
Do you remember where you said I don't know how you have
done it? Well, my dear friend, I am who I am and have gotten
myself to where I am with the grace of God and the angels he
has chosen to watch over me. I live my life with that gratitude
and passion. Take care my friend and may God be with you."

Totti finally responds to Salina with a short but sweet excuse as he writes:

"Hello, my dear Salina. I'm sorry I was absent but work was busy. Here are your answers to your questions you recently asked to me:

Do you play a strategic game of chess?
I am not really good in the game of chess but you can teach me.

Do you enjoy picnics and walks in the woods?
Yes, it is a wonderful adventure.
Do you kayak?
Yes, I love water.

Do you like hockey?
Yes, I enjoy any kind of sport.

Do you like mudding 4x4 or adventures?
Yes, I enjoy getting down and dirty!

Do you like baseball?
I love baseball.

Do you play a game of pool or darts?
Yes, I like both.

What is your favorite alcohol?
I always enjoy a glass of red wine, white wine or champagne.

Do you smoke?
No, I do not smoke anything.

If you could only take one more trip anywhere in the world: where would it be and why?
I'd love to visit the Bahamas, because I have never been there. I hear it is a wonderful place to spend holidays.

Do you like animals?
Yes, I love all animals.

Would you help me write more books?
Yes, of course I will help.

Do you feel our story is a book?
Yes and it's more than a book!

Can you leave work alone when you go out to play?
Yes, of course I can.

Do you enjoy the snow?
Yes I do.

Do you enjoy walking in the rain?
Yes, I love to walk in the rain.

Have you ever danced in the rain?
Give it a try and see how free your soul will feel.

What time is it where you are now?
It is 11:36 am.

"Do you have any more questions my dearest Salina? I look forward to your next email. Oh, I have missed your messages sweetie! I'm very sorry for not replying you early enough. Please forgive me. I just tried to call you but you didn't pick up. I miss you so much sweetie and you never left my thoughts. Please pick up your phone? I don't know what I have done that I deserve a second chance. I lost one and yet I found another angel. How did I become so lucky? I trusted my instincts and got only you from that market and you turned gold. My instincts still direct me to move ahead with her in my journey. I really thank my God. I mean I ask for something good and he gives me the best. Hiding from the whole past, rains and snow, for I may be reminded of some memories, trying to forget yet I won't let go. Walking through a crowded street, I could still hear my own heartbeat. So many people around this world my dear, tell me, where do I find someone like you? Lol. Please take me to your heart, take me to your soul, and show me that wonders can be true? They say, nothing lasts forever, we are only here today, and love is now or never. Please bring me far away? Give me your hand and hold me, show me what love is, maybe I haven't got a clue. You can just be my guardian star. Take my hands before I am too old. Lol. I could go be with some friends to have fun, but they don't really comprehend. I don't need too much talking, without saying anything: all I need is some one who makes me want to sing. Salina, you do a great job on that. I have written a song I would sing for you when I get to you. In less than few weeks I would handover and come see you. Would you mind picking this old man from the airport? Lol. We should really take this to another level. Let me hear the voice of an angel. Be warned I have been told I have an unsorted accent, but sexy. Lol. Now I can hardly get you out of my mind. Be safe my Angel."

Salina replies: "Hello Totti, I am sorry, but I was in a no reception area today when you called because it never reached me. Did you get my voice mail when you called me? I also do not answer numbers that I do not recognize: sorry, it's a safety thing. My number is wireless, not a land line +56723469601. I would like to talk to you over the phone. Maybe we will get the chance again. ☺ Work is absolutely crazy this week with the back to school appointments so I get home every night around 10:00 pm. It is always a pleasure to hear from you my long distance friend. I must ask you isn't your God . . . my God? As I read your email the other night, new questions arose when you spoke of hiding from the whole past, rains and snow? Is this why you are single my friend? Have you not let anyone close enough to know your soul? Has the distance been a safety net? Isn't it funny how we have allowed our souls to be free in the electronic world but guard ourselves in the everyday reality world? A country singer sings it best when he sings I'm going to walk out in the rain, and I'm going to wash away the pain and I'm going to let it go. I have allowed you to become a part of my world as truth by letting you become my friend on this website. My life is an open book. Yours on the other hand brings many questions. Your life appears to be hidden and subdued as I appear to be your only friend? Why is this? If you were to reverse places, how would you look at me if I had absolutely no connections? You appear to me as an intelligent man, so I ask again my friend isn't there someone like me in your world already? I have become addicted to your emails and have prayed to my God for safety and assurance that we are truth. Yes, Totti, dancing in the rain frees the child inside of all of us. ☺Be safe my friend. I hope you are doing well. I will write tomorrow my dear long distance friend."

Salina recognizes the challenge and strategy of this electronic affair that is visible at times during her communication with Totti. She tries to get him to call her cell phone because the call could be traced but Totti continues to avoid the issue. Salina hesitates for awhile before she sends her email to Totti. She gets a response within an hour from him that reads:

"Good evening my beauty. Now I am having an affair with my computer. Lol. I go to bed looking at it and wake to run to it. Lol. How soon shall my love take over? Hehehe. When I run to the pc and finally see your name on it, a big smile escapes my mouth and I feel that I have another chance to build the dream life. And yeah it seems like it has started. Lol. So you asked me more questions and I will answer you now with truth Salina.

I must ask you isn't your God . . . my God?
"Yes Salina, we do believe in same GOD."

Is this why you are single my friend?
"Well, the reason why I was single till I met you is because no one as ever reaches my heart the way I feel for you."

Have you not let anyone close enough to know your soul?
"I have but what I get back is heart breaks."

Has the distance been a safety net?
"Yes. I bless GOD so far so good along with you on this project. Lol."

If you were to reverse places, how would you look at me if I had absolutely no connections?
"I don't really know how to answer this but I believe GOD wants us together and we finally met."

You appear to me as an intelligent man, so I ask you again my friend, isn't there someone like me in your world already?
"No! No! No! No one but you I swear! I found you and I'm 100% honest with you! I want you forever my princess."

"Salina, there is no mission without a vision, so the dream here is what we have in common. Maybe I should just tell you how a typical day in the dream life looks like for a picture here. I wake up to her fresh breath on my neck, make her breakfast and bring to bed so I can get paid with a kiss early in the morning Lol. We probably go in shower together and get ready for work together. Then I would love to drop her at work before I return to my home office to work my job. I would love her to distract me most of the time while I work, I can chase her round the house, and in fact a good dip in the pool at midnight would be fun. But who says such life can't be anymore? It takes will and zeal above all things. Who says I can't have the good life, I know I want it and will get it. After all people do almost anything for money, but for me, I will do everything for love. It is about compromises, sacrifices and forgiveness. How hard could that be? You only need to remember everyday that if you can't forgive her, you don't deserve her Lol. ☺ I think life can be sweet if you really want it to. I am still lucky to get your attention. When you feel it, you can know it because love needs no map, for it can find its way blindfolded. I just want to make my way to the depth of your heart first and see what it feels like. Many guys always seem to wonder what it takes to get a girl. Like, what do they have to do to make a girl notice them? Guys have to realize that they have to be sweet, caring, gentle, and honest and still have that sweet little thing about them that drives any girl crazy: and that's reaching her heart. No matter how much you try, if you don't reach her heart, it won't ever be worth-while.

"My dear, I am on my rig for supplies and fixtures for the next few days, but you would be the first person I see once I am off sea. Lol. But before then, everyday I shall send my thoughts your way until I can behold and stare in those sincere big brown eyes. I think more luck is this opportunity to know in-depth about you so when we finally meet I don't think we will be strangers. Lol. I get to talk to my ma and my son everyday. You will like my son. He looks much like his mom and everybody says he is the sweetest boy. Lol. I will be waiting impatiently for your next email note. Write soon, ok?"

Salina laughs as she writes:
"Ha-ha Totti . . . I am also having an electronic affair. ☺
     The last thing I do before I close my eyes each night is too write to you my dear man on this little electronic tablet, and then I check it when I awake to see if you have read it. Oh, my! What an addiction! LOL. I think our time is many hours apart. It is now 10:26 pm Wednesday night here in the northeast so what time would it be where you are? I think you are an amazing writer. I have never met anyone who can write with the same technique as I do. I often feel you are a mirror reflection. Crazy. Huh? Would you help me write more books? Do you feel our story is a good book?

Have you thought about what our days would be like without this connection? How unique that we are each other's fascination? Do you think we could be this way in reality day to day? What if when we finally meet we do not feel the same attraction as we do when we write? There is so much to think about. Is this whole thing real or is it all a dream? Is this all going to disappear like it never happened? Lol. So my dear friend, you said you talk to your mom and son everyday? How often do you see them? It must be difficult to be far away? I do not know that way of life because I raised and lived for my children and see my grandchildren almost daily in passing whereas we all live here on the mountain. My parents have both rested. You are blessed to still have your mom, I miss mine everyday. L My dear man, I am sleepy so I will close my eyes with the pleasant thoughts of you and pray you are safe."

It is early morning when Salina hears her cell phone beep and lets her know Totti just sent her an email. With eyes half open she checks to see what Totti's email says:

"Good morning sweetie, my own Joy, You are my ray of hope, just like sunshine, brightening my world, I just can't get my eyes off of your picture that I got from social media. It only seemed like yesterday you came my way like an angel without wings to rock my world. To give meaning to the beautiful life I had that had no meaning and essence of family? Only because of you, I feel the presence and will of family. Like I said I am not God so I don't know how tomorrow will be for us, but like I said, we are only here today and my feelings are thus! Without fear or remorse I have embraced you, and I can tell you, I will not only love you, but also love those you love as if they were my own. I am an instinctive person my dear and I get this gut feeling that you have been the one taking care of people around you but I know it is time for you to be taken care of, so please give me the job! Lol. I want to have the best job in this world which is to put a permanent smile on your face. ☺ Lol . . . I have taken down my profile I am leaving it to my fate and destiny. I hope you do yours too if you believe in this friendship. Since the Lord says as a man thinks, so he is, so put our trust in motion and leave the rest to heaven. Like I say, you win me only because you have always been you. I mean if I fell in love with you for beauty how long shall I travel to see more beauty? If I did for smiles, I would still see more but if I do for you being you, then no worries as that is who no one else can ever be. Lol. Seriously, I think we are lucky to have this medium to explore each other's mind here: though I still can never resist your sincere smile. You asked me if I've thought about what our days would be like without this connection. I know God has something good in store for us. He is not an evil God but a loving God. And when we are in each other's arms, that love will be more amazing than what we have now. Even though we are far apart, my heart will always be with you. As long as we have the memories and as long as we have hope then tomorrow awaits. As long as we are still in love, each day is never a waste and the waiting will prove worthwhile.

"You asked me if I think we could be this way in reality day to day. We had never met but the love we feel is so big and true already and could only become complete by meeting each other.

"You asked me what if when we finally meet we do not feel the same attraction as we do when we write. Well, we started at forever and will end at never. Sweetie, it's our turn and it's our turn to make each other happy.

"You asked how often do you I see my ma and son? I see them 2 times in a year. Yes, it is difficult to be away but he understands and like I told you, he is a smart boy.

"We all fight in this world, go to war and have condemnation hence we forget that we can never leave without each other, seriously if we think it deep down then we will know and remember our purposes, I mean what would a police man do without criminals? What would the rich do without the poor? What would the Christians do without the opposition?

What would the racists do without different races? We were all created for each other and that is one way to realize God himself wants a balance here. ☺ Lol. Like the prayer says we had better be wise to quickly change what we can and accept what we can't and pray for serenity to know the difference for the only constant thing in life is change. I told my son about you yesterday and he says I have good taste. Now he has been another factor who pushed me to date again. He promised me he did not need me to be unmarried to care for him but he always said he wanted someone to look up to as a mother since his mother died when he was too young. He also said only if I knew he would leave me one day for his own family so I should be smart enough and get myself a life partner according to him. He is a sweet boy, he talks so funny and like a 40 year old too. He's so grown up.

"Please take good care of yourself and have a wonderful day. I will be thinking of you and I can't wait to hold you soon, with God's approval."

Salina is feeling frustrated with Totti as she answers his last letter:

"Hello Totti, it is now 9:13 pm Thursday here and I am feeling like it would be nice to hear your voice instead of typing. I still do not understand our time difference? If it is 9:30 pm here so what time would it be there? Today I sent you a chat text: did you get it? I am confused about you saying I had a picture on a singles social media website? Quite sometime ago I did a profile questionnaire to find out my personality traits and then I printed it. It was amazing because it nailed my personality. Lol. I never went back on the sight after that, so I totally forgot about it. Did you look at the date because I think it was about 7 years ago? Lol. Is that how you found me on this website? So, do tell me what your days are like. What time do you awake? Walk me through a day in your life. Tell me all the little details like your habits, choice of meals, daily activity, evenings, at bedtime: just paint me the picture of you in 24 hours. Oh and I am thankful you are not a smoker because neither am I. And different wines are my favorite cocktails. ☺ Again we have common character elements. I look forward to your email my electronic affair. ☺ Take care and be safe! Chat soon!"

As Salina hits send, she notices there is another email from Totti so she opens and reads:

"Salina, it's the end of the day now. I always wake up 5:00 am then make some tea, take my bath then start my day with reading your email till 5:45 am before finally leaving for work 6:00 am. I was thinking about you, as usual. I want you to know how much I sincerely love the times we've spent talking. It means so much to me. It truly seems like I've known you forever and I honestly can't imagine life without you now. There will be no looking back, no second thoughts and no regrets. I want you and need only you and I believe that love will only grow stronger. Do not be scared sweetie: sometimes life hits you with unexpected things that take you totally by surprise. All I can say is you're the best surprise life has given me and your capacity for love, caring, and understanding never ceases to amaze me. I've truly been blessed by finding you, Yes, that social media website was where I found your picture a few years back but I wasn't an active member on the site. You were the match they sent to me but I couldn't message you because I wasn't a paid member. L Then I told a friend about the site and he asked me to see if I could see your profile on this website. Suddenly I found it but wasn't sure if it was you so I had to write to you in the other email. I already took my profile down because it's of no use to me anymore. I should have told you this, there's this special love that I have deep within my heart. That love is now only just for you. It is far greater than this planet, galaxy or universe. I wish I could show you how much you really mean to me. If I could let you feel how much I do really love you in a kiss or hug, you would only feel the surface of the love that I have for you. The only time when I can show you how much I do really love you is when we are together. For then you will see and understand how much I love you. You can hear the language of my love for you by listening to my heart because it will speak to you. You can taste the sweetest of it in a kiss and you can feel it in a hug. When you look deep into my eyes then you will see how great my love for you is. You will also know and see that it's no lie! If I could describe the love that I have for you I would use lyrics of love songs and even the sonnets of famous poets. It would be amazing and yet impossible to believe because the love that I have for you is real, unconditional, everlasting and indescribable! You've had my heart and soul from the day we met and you will have it forever. I know as time goes by my heart and love for you will keep on growing stronger, brighter and bigger. You are all mine, as I am all yours. Although we have two different bodies, minds and souls, we have one and the same beautiful heart. This is my unconditional love for you, from me to you. Sweetie with all my heart, body, mind and soul you are my life, my world and everything. Distance may keep us apart, but you will always and forever be embedded deep within my heart. I love you! Salina, the truth is. I have lived for a long time, responsible for and dependent upon no one, answering to no one and committed to no one except myself. During this period of my life, I considered the world mine for the taking and truly believed that I was living life to the fullest. Then you came into the picture and all of a sudden I realized that I was deceiving myself. I find that my life is not all that I thought it was. In fact, it is terribly lacking in many things, the foremost being love. Now, through some great fortune, I have found that love and along with it the one person who can make my life truly complete. You are that person, and I have somehow fallen in love with you. To be honest, I never thought I would ever utter those words but now they come forth effortlessly and with great sincerity. I'll be forever being grateful to you for showing me just how shallow my life was. At last, I have a chance to give it depth and purpose."

Salina feels bewildered when she gets emails from Totti where he appears to be truly sincere and honest. There are times during this electronic affair that she feels like she is writing to different people. "Oh," she gasps, "Sometimes I think he's a real person and then other times I think someone else is playing me. How much is real and how much of this is a copy and paste response? I'd like to meet the person if he turns out to be real," Salina mumbles as she responds to Totti's letter.

"My dearest Totti: Your words of self expression never cease to amaze me. I believe in you and also with you that our self sufficiency has never been a weakness of either of ours. Your words below explain a lot to me. Your honesty appears deep in your words spoken my friend where you explain how you have lived your life with little depth and purpose.

I can feel compassion for the little boy inside of you who is setting himself free so that he can now soar with the eagles as an earned position in life. You are ready now my dear man for your next great journey. My caring soul, you do not need a woman to complete you for you will now walk forward and wear your crown as a mature man. There is no doubt now that you are ready to walk side by side with a woman equivalent to you such as myself. Such a relationship of any title with this level of honor is the greatest gift to man so that the legacy of true love may be carried onto the reproduced generation known as family. Without a doubt, this is the definition of what you called depth and purpose.

"So, my friend, please tell me more about your everyday habits? I can picture you awake at 5:00 am and preparing for your day. I also enjoy tea, but am usually drinking it in the evening because my coffee is my wake up beverage. Won't you please walk me through a complete day in your life? Tell me all of the little details like, habits, choice of meals, your daily activity, your evenings, your bedtime: just paint me the picture of you in 24 hours? I'm silly, huh? Moments make my everyday with so many little things that go often without

77

notice. My morning consists of waking, feeding the fish, cat and dog, then grabbing my coffee and sitting out on the deck listening to the sounds of nature like the waterfall, the birds, etc . . . It is preparation time for me to kick in high gear and go face the public and all of my daily responsibilities. Each day never brings the same people or events to my life: therefore there is never a dull moment. ☺ My responsibilities do not end after work because I then go home to do the laundry, cooking, cleaning and always with the sound of music. Then I jump in the shower to so call wash the public off. Lol. When all is said and done, I relax with a glass of wine or a cup of tea and sit watching the fish in the aquarium and cuddle with the dog and cat. That is usually when I am on my tablet writing to you, knowing I will close my eyes with your vision on my mind. Good night my dear Totti. Be safe."

Salina is bewildered when Totti replies quickly with:
"Sweetie, there are just some things that words cannot describe. The feeling I have when I read your messages, when I think about you, and when I dream about you, is amazing. I've never felt that before in my life. I think that you're a wonderful person and without you there is no me. I don't know where I would be right now. My love for you has grown so much over the past couple of months. I think back to when I first wrote you an email, I would have never imagined that we would be where we are today. It's just going to keep getting better. I don't think that our love will ever fade or wither. I'll always be there for you and when you need someone to talk to I hope you come to me. I'll be your best friend. So once again I say, all of you. My life is perfect with you in it. So, I thank you. You have opened up new and exciting doors for us that I can't wait to explore with you. My soul is set on fire with desire to hold you and kiss you. You have become my very best friend and my wanted lover. So, make no mistake, Sweetie, this is love because you're the one who holds the key to my heart. You always say what I need to hear. You make

me feel special, like I'm your one and only. You make me feel like I'm a star in the sky lighting up your life. We're a perfect match. Thinking of you fills me with a wonderful feeling. I'll always love you Salina."

It is a holiday weekend and Salina is away camping with her friends. She decides to share her story with her friend of 20 years to get her opinion about Totti and what little information about him she has. Totti is now leaving comments on Salina's social media website and friends are asking about him. Salina hides his remarks because she is not ready to go public and explain him within her circle of family and friends. Before she goes to sleep she writes to Totti:

"Hello my friend, how are you tonight? It is a holiday and I am away for the weekend with friends at a music festival at Tiny Point Campground on the ocean. I will return tomorrow to work as usual. How is your weekend? What is your world like today? My understanding is that you are in a present world of seclusion due to your job? My prayers go to you while you are away. Your chosen career challenge at this time appears to be the character of your father who believed also that he could conquest the world and take the success as international conqueror. ☺ So for you my friend of paternal genetic reflection, I say God speed and watch over you until you return home safely.

"It is midnight now and here I am again getting ready to close my eyes with wonderful thoughts of you my dear Totti. Yes, you are special my friend. You are like my one and only because somehow you found the key to open my soul. I am enjoying the dream! ☺No one has gone there before. How has this happened? My soul has been unobtainable to others and yet you walked through the closed door as though you were a ghost. Why is that? I feel that we are both blessed to have found this type of connection. As you have said before the soul connection we have with each other will always keep us together and is the one thing no one can take from us. No one else can have that part of our hearts. Just as the spirits connected through this medium, so I hope God will guide our journey. Until we chat again be safe my dearest friend."

Salina feels like something is a little strange and that what Totti writes back to her is a copy and paste from some old poetry:

"My dear Salina, you became so honorable in my eyes, like a precious gem, counted with extremely good intellectual reasoning makes me emotionally struck and speechless.

The above-stated utterances and delightful contemplation of something worthy is inexpressible on my part because I was made to understand such sublime and noble qualities are inherent with you. I am very serious now in telling you that I can no longer endure such extreme anxiety and sleepless nights that I am experiencing right of this moment. Because since I met you I felt I was living in a new and wonderful world, full of love. And the sun is brighter, the pastures became greener and everything I do was magnificent. You should inculcate and instill in your mind that I cherish you so much. Such love, like everything, deserves to be given much attention and care in order to grow more and more and I promise you this, from this day forth I will love you forever don't' ever doubt that. I will never want anyone else's touch but yours: you make me feel like I am the only man in the world. You are the only woman in the world as far as I am concerned. You are my heart and soul. I feel as though we are meant to be together, that we have been brought together by God. I have always believed that I had a soul mate out there and I am sure that is you, I see it every time I read your email and I feel it when you hold me in your arms. Salina, I love you. I love you more than my life, more than my world. I love you more and more each day and that is the most wonderful feeling any man can ever hope to experience. One last thing before I go. I have wanted to tell you something, but have not been able to bring myself to do so. I love you Salina."

Salina is a little puzzled by all of this desperate love chatter and is unsure where any of this discussion is going. She is sure it is all not detrimental to her real world but she is not sure if any of this is real in Totti's life and does not want any harm to come to either of them. Salina is sincere when she writes to him:

"Hello Totti. Now I am really confused. Why are you saying you can no longer endure such extreme anxiety and sleepless nights that you are experiencing right at this moment? Why did you say you are very serious now in telling me that? Have you not been serious up to now? Are you alright? Are you saying goodbye to me but that you'll always love me in your heart? Help me to understand, please? Maybe, I do not want to let this adventure go! As strange as this all appears, I believe we have been brought together for a reason even if it is for a deep friendship. Many people never find that."

Totti's reply is another deep love letter and as Salina reads it she is saddened by the possibility that this whole scenario is not real. She would like it to be but she has recognizes the artificial elements of this electronic affair. Salina's anticipation is increasing as she reads Totti's email:

"Sweetie it's 6:30 pm on Wednesday here, I want to tell you today how good I feel about us and our future, I'm so satisfied with all we have together, and I'm sure that those feelings will last that I'll cherish you through a lifetime of beautiful tomorrows. I want you to know how pleased I am to be a part of your life, how much it means to me to know I'll always be in love with you and only you and I really had a sleepless night, moving here and there on my bed and thinking about you because you are irresistible to me and I don't know how anyone could let you go. I know I never will and you have completed me in more ways than you could ever imagine. The love you have given to me is sometimes so hard to believe that I still have to pinch myself to make sure it's really in my life.

Ever since you came into my life with this heavenly made gift called love, I have noticed so many changes in my left alone world. You made me believe again that love comes to those who knows and listens to the music of love.

"Seriously, Salina, I love you because I have never been loved by anyone the way you love me. I feel like a complete man. I love your patient manner, your generous nature. You have touched my life in so many ways and you made me understand that life is all about appreciation and understanding but must be appreciated first before understanding. I want to make this promise based on the love that you have shown me and the things you have done to keep my hopes alive, Sweetie, today, I declare my love for you alone, no one but you and it's from the bottom of my heart. I promise to be there for you in good and bad times because you are worth dying for. I love you so very much, Salina always and forever! I'm so very thankful to share this with you!

"Remember I love you sweetie. Don't work too hard. This evening the weather is expected to be warmer than usual. You are a special woman with unique and intriguing qualities that drive my desire for you far beyond any imagination. I can't wait to grow old with you to one day reminisce of the years we shared together sharing emails. Just the thought of offering my total heart and spending my life cherishing every moment with you brings these incredible emotions to me I have never experienced before. A wise man once told me when it is real, you will know. I know that I love you Salina!"

Salina is half asleep when she answers Totti:
"Just call me night owl. Lol. Again at midnight on Wednesday, I find myself engaged in a love affair with this little hand held electronic box. Oh, my . . . no wonder I am tired in the am.

Ahhh . . . but the element of captivity is sooo worth my time. Lol. Ok Totti my dear, I am trying to make light of a very intense subject . . . sleep! ☺ No more sleepless nights of anticipation and anxiety because it is not healthy. Besides, I am not going to disappear because friends always are there for each other. Lol. I want you to be rested, healthy and very alert with your environment so that you can succeed at your goal. You are responsible for your success with safety so that you can be prepared for your future journey. I am there for you my friend, so please use no energy within the negative mode to allow any vulnerability to surface. Be submissive to God's guidance so that your mission can be completed safely. Do not display any weakness to evil by exhaustion because it will thrive with your insecurities. You and I are now one and have been intertwined to become soul mates and friends who will always love, honor and cherish each other until death do us part. You have entered my life and already captured the part of me that no one else has ever been able to: that my friend is my soul. And I believe if this is real and true then as the spiritual world brought us together, so will that world protect and guide us always. Don't you think?"

Totti answers Salina immediately with more poetic mail: "I promise . . . to me, you're a rose that should be protected from thorns around lest they prick you. You're an angel that shouldn't be hurt. You're also honey that should be covered against contaminants. By the grace of God, I'm ready to do whatever it takes to make you happy, I promise. I love you. You complete me Salina. I could never imagine what it would be like if we were to lose each other. I don't even want to think about it. All I want to think of is you because there is so much I want to tell you, a lot has been running through my head lately. I keep thinking about the future, about life, and what I want out of it. I keep thinking about us and what this relationship means to me. I keep thinking about these things and I realize they go hand in hand. This relationship is my future: it's what I want out of life. I want to grow old with you. I want to experience this wonderful love forever and ever, I want to see you walk around our house in a big t-shirt with your hair down and catch me staring at how gorgeous you are. I want you to pull the covers off me at night and then I have to get even closer, if it's possible, to you to keep warm. I want to rub lotion all over your body because you lay out in the sun too long. I want to hold you when you cry and smile with you when you smile. I want to fall asleep every night with you in my arms. I want you to fall asleep on my chest listening to the beat of my heart and know it beats for you I want you to be the first thing I see when I wake up and the last thing I see when I go to sleep. I want to see your bad morning hair: I think it will be so cute. I want to sit on the beach with you and watch the sun set, and I want all the people who pass us to envy the love that we obviously have for each other. I want to take your hand for the rest of my life. I want to spend all night, and maybe the next day, making love to you with an undying passion (sorry to be so blunt). I want to be eighty years old and still make out with you like a little college kid. I want to cook a meal with you and us totally ruin it and end up doing take out. I want to sit there talking to you for hours about nothing at all but in the same time everything or maybe we won't talk at all and just grin at each other realizing how lucky we are. I want to lay with you in front of a fireplace and keep the heat going long after the fire goes out. I want to take trips with you to places we've never been and experience them together. I want our friends to come over and get totally jealous because they don't share a love like we do. I want to be walking into a store with you. I want us to run outside in the rain and act like total kids getting completely soaked, and when we come back in stripping down to nothing as we stumble into the bedroom, or the kitchen counter, or the balcony, or the dining room table, or an office desk, or the shower, which ever one we feel like at the time. Lol. I want it to take your breath away every time I say, I love you because you know it's coming from the heart, well, I'll let your imagination finish the rest, Lol. I want to love you and be with you for at least forever if not a little longer. I couldn't really express in words what I'm feeling right now so I decided to share with you some of the images and thoughts that have been running through my head. I just want you to know that I had never found someone I wanted to spend the rest of my life with until I met you. I really am crazy about you, everything about you Salina. I love you!"

As Salina and Kasey discuss this electronic affair and if it is real or not, both girls agree that there are so many inconsistencies with Totti's information that it might be time to do some more research. Kasey suggests to Salina that she should become a photo detective and trace the pictures that Totti sent to her. The girl's imaginations run wild as they laugh about who this man really might be. They are surprised when they copy and paste his picture into an electronic search bar and immediately get results.

"Wow," says Kasey. "Do you think he knows you can trace him?"

Salina replies, "I'll bet this isn't his first online scam. Obviously he has been playing others because look at his profile."

Kasey giggles, "Salina, when are you going to tell him you found these other bogus profiles with him?"

Salina laughs as she says, "I don't know when the story will end but one thing is for sure Kasey, this book has to have an ending. Nobody's getting hurt and I love the challenge! Instead of playing electronic chess all summer, I took on this scam challenge that appeared on my social media page. My friends said they were getting these types of letters in their other message boxes too, so I decided to discard all of them but one and play it. Whew! What a story it is, huh?"

"It is all too crazy that this kind of thing is happening all over the place now!" Kasey exclaims. "I checked my social media mail and found three of them from female and male strangers so I told my daughter and friends to be aware also. How dangerous could these situations be? It's all so crazy!"

Salina sighs as she answers Kasey with, "Do you want to know what's so sad about this whole thing? There is a real person working these kinds of scams and it makes you wonder if they have feelings when they do this, huh? Well Kasey, time will tell. It is so easy to get caught up in something like this. We will both just have to watch to see where it goes and how it ends. Lol. Let's grab lunch before we have to get back to work."

The Queen

Chapter ~ 5 ~

~ Two Conclusions: Victory and Loss ~

S alina and Totti appear to be playing the other with the match of minds in this electronic affair. The challenge and strategy of the game has now become evident with both players. The game is on! Who will conclude the challenge with a victory and who will feel the loss?

Salina is busy at work when she goes into the office and she notices Totti has opens a reality chat conversation that startles her. Totti does not realize that Salina has discovered some hidden truths about her friend from her electronic affair.
Totti:
"Hello Salina. I love you more than myself. ☺"

Salina:
"Hi Totti, how is your day going?"

Totti:
"My day is going well. I've been thinking about you."
"It is 12:20 am here right now."

Salina:
"Really, it is 4:20 pm here and I am waiting for the next client to show up."

Totti:
"Oh, ok."

Salina:
"What's happening with you?"

Totti:
"I hope you aren't too tired."

Salina Toya:
"I rarely get too tired. Lol. Guess I don't know any better. Lol."

Totti:
"Are you serious sweetie?"

Salina:
"Absolutely, I believe sleep is overrated. Lol."

Totti:
"Oh, okay sweetie. Lol.
Salina, I love you so much."

Salina:
"So Totti, what are things like in your world?"

Totti:
"There's nothing so special about here sweetie, thinking about you makes everything looks great. Did you receive my email today?"

Salina:
"Totti, I'll check my email and get back to you."

Salina:
"I'm camping this weekend for the holiday weekend. How about you? Do you get the holiday weekend to play?"

Totti:
"Things have to be done here. Work! Work! Work!
I need to finish as soon as possible, so not much time for camping.
Hey Sweetie. Are you still there? I guess you left me alone here.
I love you Salina."

Totti pushes the buzzer a few times to try to connect to Salina on voice chat. BUZZ!!! BUZZ!!! BUZZ!!! BUZZ!!!

Salina:
"Silly. So alone? Hmmmm. Do you mind being alone?
Myself? I love my own company. Lol."

Totti:
"Salina, I am never alone because I read your emails always."

Salina:

"I did get your emails today and as always I read them intensely."

Totti:

"You mean so much to me sweetie."

Salina:

"Do you have any new pictures of yourself my dear loving Totti?

Salina:

I went on your website page and there are no pics?"

Totti:

"Yes I do but it in my phone on my memory card. I don't really like posting pictures. I am really shy. Lol."

Salina:

"Oh, you can send them to my phone via text @ 54271286660 That would be awesome! After all, it is 50/50 right?"

Totti:

"I wish that you were here or that I were there, or that we were together anywhere."

Salina:

"You get to see all of my pics on this website with myself, my family and my business. Am I right?"

Totti:

"Yes. I guess so. Sweetie you will see my pictures on my ipad when I get back. I have a lot of pictures to show you. Okay?"

Salina:

"When you get back from where?"

Totti:
"Yes sweetie. What do you think?"

Salina:
"Totti, I forgot to tell you that my friend Sara and I went camping. She had a friend there from California that worked on the ships where you are. What a coincidence, huh?
It was great to hear the validation of your environment."

Totti:
"Oh that's nice."

Salina:
"Yeah, her friend has a high dollar camp bus and travels all of the music festivals. He says he is retired from working as a computer tech on the ships that went to Dubai when he lived in Sacramento."

Totti:
"Oh? Ok. Sweetie what do you think about the pictures you've asked for?"

Salina:
"Totti, I just think I would enjoy feeling closer by looking at your picture, don't you think? You know what it's like. A picture says a thousand words. Right?"

Totti:
"Oh, Okay sweetie, I will send you some couple of pictures."

Salina:
"So, speaking of the music festival, do you play any instruments?"

Totti:
"Yes. I play the drums and guitar a little."

Salina:
"That's great! Do you ever play with others? I think it is a lot of fun to sing harmony. I hope to pick up the DoBro."

Totti:
"I'm also good playing the piano too."

Salina:
"Totti, when you send pics by text message just let me know with a text so I know it is you, ok?"

Totti:
"Oh, okay sweetie."

Salina:
"That's great! Music is where the heart is. I think those who always have a song are never lonely."

Totti:
"I will email them so you could have them in your emails and not mistakenly delete them."

Salina:
"Totti, please send them by text if you can because then I can text you back???"

Totti:
"Okay sweetie. If I could have one wish it would just be this, I could take you to my soul and show you all the love there is."

Salina:
"I believe one's soul shines through one's exterior by their actions and reactions. Don't you think?"

Totti:
"Yes. Close together or far apart, you're forever in my heart. I love you in the morning, in the middle of the day, in the hours we are together and the hours we are away."

Salina:
"So, you are reciting poetry now?
Hmmm . . . when do you sleep if it is 12:20 am where you are right now?"

Totti:
"Oh, I can fall asleep anytime."

Salina:
"Silly, aren't you tired?"

Totti:
"I feel great right now because I get to chat with you."

Salina:
"I have a question for you my dear . . ."

Totti:
"You can ask me anything."

Salina:
"I have learned some of your strengths Totti so now I am curious What are your insecurities?"

Totti:
"Well my insecurities lies on GOD. I really don't worry about anything until it happens. I need to sleep now. I Love you sweetie. Will you email me soon?"

Totti signs out and Salina emails Totti before she leaves work to go home for the night.

"Hello my long distance electronic affair. How are you this Thursday evening? I just wanted to tell you how much I cherish your emails Totti. The man you describe during the past few months is absolutely amazing. I will always hold you in my heart no matter how far apart we are. I enjoyed our instant chat today because I felt like we were sitting there together just talking. ☺ That makes us so real in the everyday mode. Don't you think? I look forward to you sending me a new picture of yourself with a text so I can have you close to me all the time. Then when ever I think of you, I can look at your picture and feel that you are near me. You display a remarkable man. Please stay safe. I'm sending hugs to you."

Later that night Salina gets a reply from Totti that reads:

"Salina how was I to know that you were watching me sleep? I awoke to see you lying there and just then you smiled and said hello. That just melted me. I wish with all of my heart on this Thursday night that I could wake to your beautiful eyes for the rest of my life. Every day I think of you and it makes me happier and happier knowing that I can spend the rest of my life with you. I know I will never have to worry about losing you because I know that you will never leave me. I know it when I look into your eyes. Sweetie, I tried to text my pictures to you but my cell phone will not allow me to so I decided to email them to you. I hope you like them. I am not a picture person. Lol. I love you Salina."

Before she retires for the night, Salina answers Totti's email playfully even though she knows the game is nearing an end.

"Totti, I can only imagine that I kiss your cheek teasingly and catch a half awake grin. I sigh with contentment as I dream of being the luckiest woman around. ☺ Hmmmm. Why is that my darling Totti? My dear man, I am embracing the warm thoughts of having someone like you in my life someday. I will hold your memory in my heart and soul forever. ☺ Take care of yourself my friend."

The King

Chapter ~ 6 ~

~ The Conquest: Triumph and Defeat ~

Totti feels threatened as he recognizes Salina's change of attitude. He desperately tries to keep Salina within his reach by telling her that she will always hold a place in his heart. Salina reciprocates that he will never be forgotten. Then proudly she announces to Totti that the game has ended with a checkmate as she has maneuvered him into a position from which he cannot escape, bringing the game to a victorious conclusion.

Salina feels disappointed as she prepares to separate this imaginary relationship and bring herself back to reality. She wonders how this endeavor will really end. As she writes Totti a parting letter she gets an email from him that reads:

"Sweetie, a beautiful new month makes me love you more. Selena, as this new month of September 2013 begins may this month bring you satisfaction with peace and joy. May all the desires of your heart be granted for this is the beginning of new things in your life so stay strong, be positive and fulfill your dreams. You are the only one who can make me happy with your love and affection. Since I have met you I have noticed that life is worth living. I live mine for you. You have stolen me from me because alone I can be lost. So please do not let the distance between us become larger. Each day is more wonderful that the previous one as I know that I will see you soon. The further you will go from me, the more I will love you. A heart truly in love never loses hope but always believes in the promise of love no matter how long the time and how far the distance. There are so many ways I want to tell you that I really love you, my sweetie. My feelings for you are true and pure, I love you and I will always love you. Loving you is something I love to do. I am so wonderfully blessed to have you in my life. Salina, you will forever be loved and never forgotten. You will always have my heart no matter how far from me you are. I know in my soul that we will never be apart because our souls are bonded by a love that knows no end. I love you now and I will love you always!"

Salina hesitates for a moment after reading Totti's email. "Hmmm, I think he avoids everything and pretends like this communication between us will continue forever," she mutters: "Won't he be surprised when he reads this!" As she hits send, Salina thinks about the letter she just wrote to him:

"My dearest Totti: yes, a new month brings blessings and reflections. I wish for you many as you fulfill the desires of your heart and remain safe in your life's journey. Your character will forever be loved and never, ever forgotten. Your soul has made a lifetime impression with mine and you will always hold a piece of my heart no matter how far from me you are. I am thinking of you Totti and adoring the man that you display.

"My dear friend, I now have some real confessions. In the beginning of our electronic communications when you asked to be my friend, I allowed you to enter my world with hesitation and skepticism. Once I did, I became addicted to the challenge regarding the match of the minds. As I became engulfed in the ambience, I played each move as though it were a game of chess. It is my favorite strategy game. Each move played was exciting even though I felt many of yours were false and repetitious. Let me explain the final moves in a game of chess by definition.

   a). Check: to stop opponent, to prevent further action or to place under attack.
   b). Checkmate: an act or instance of maneuvering the opponent's leader into a check from which it cannot escape bringing the game to a conclusion.
   c). Stalemate: any position or situation in which no action can be taken or progress made: therefore to bring to a standstill.

My dear friend let us conclude our game results in a stalemate. Be safe my friend. May God watch over you?"☹

Salina does not know what she feels about this electronic affair as she puts the pressure on Totti. She thinks this will be the last email she writes to Totti because of her confessions about what she believes has been a game. Totti, however, surprises her with another love letter that reads:

"Good morning my love, wow! I actually woke very late today. It must have been the good dream about you that kept me in there. Lol. Are you my new Mrs. Mac? Lol. I would prefer you are on reality chat today as that would make us feel closer. I really can't wait to be done here. You have given me a new perspective on so many things. I will always treasure our love and keep it safe. I have missed a lot of things like regular sailing, boat cruises, though sometimes we do that here. I miss having a woman of mine in my arms cuddling upon the couch watching movies. I miss someone talking me into going to bed. Lol. Anyway sweetie, I can't write much now. I can't believe I am still not on the Rig yet but I am really still back here. I have to run now, already I am getting a code red signal from the platform and I really do pray it is not what I think it is. I need you to know that loving you is like breathing now. Lol. Take care and I will talk to you later."

And Totti does write to Salina again explaining his day:

"Hello Sweetie, how are you? This has been a sad 24 hours here. I told you I got a distress code signal from the platform right? Only getting to the rig to find four men involved in mortal accident. We lost one today, the remaining three are undergoing treatments at the medical center. I haven't been myself for the past 24 hours. I really feel so bad. I wish I could turn back the hands of time. I will still try to write more again when I feel better. I love you sweetie."

Salina believes Totti is using his last hook for her emotions and feels it is time to call him on his game. S he says her farewell with out a good-bye:

"Dear Totti, many people wish they could turn back the hands of time, for it is said by many that hindsight is always 20/20, my friend. I am wishing you well Totti and praying your story of platform injuries is truly a fabrication. I'm sending prayers for everyone's safety. I am really sorry for you my friend. It appears to me that you have played this game giving your best. I think it is time for all this game to come to an end. My dear Totti, I found this information on another social media website. It is a profile with your name and data so I thought it would be nice to share it with you. ☺ I am sure you will enjoy it!"

Single's Profile: *Totti Rich Mac*
Male: *Single*
Age: *50-54 years*
Reading Choice: *Poetry*
Movie Choice: *Drama, Mystery and HP*
Music Choice: *gigs*
Biography:

"I love to laugh and make people smile. I am a fun loving man who wants to make the most of life and enjoy each day to the fullest. My personality is my greatest strength. My ideal woman would be one that enjoys the outdoors, laughing, playing together, and still has a romantic, compassionate side. Honesty, integrity, and communication are the values that I admire, along with loyalty, character, class and self-esteem. Life is short and often not fair, but I have grown to realize that. Life is a precious gift and everyday needs to be savored and appreciated."

SCAM Email Address: onegolddigga@lol.com

SCAM Do Not Contact! ***FAKE***

Salina shares this with Kasey and giggles with relief when she posts on Totti's social media website the information that she found online about him. Both girls chuckle as Salina announces, "Wow, Kasey, I scammed a scammer! Do you think he is surprised with the outcome? Now we know how the story ends." ☺ Then she writes one last email to Totti claiming her victory:

"Hey Totti, this is some very interesting information that I have discovered about your character: Billy Rock, Billy Rank or who ever you really are! The game is now over; Checkmate my friend!"

Salina feels sure Totti is surprised because she notices that his profile immediately disappears from the social media website leaving her only the traces of his memory. Salina sighs with sadness but relief as she closes the door on what she believes to be a potentially dangerous scam that she calls Match of Minds: Electronic Affair.

~ Epilogue ~

B
ased on true events, the identities in this story have been changed to protect the people involved. The times and dates, however, are accurate. The purpose behind the story is to share and expose the lack of truths in today's electronic communications.

A
ccess to the internet has allowed scammers to prey on the vulnerabilities of people in every age group. It is important to question everything that appears out of the ordinary. Use caution when feeling unsure or suspicious. Always question any and all abstract inquiries that may appear during electronic communications. Respond only to communications when the sender and recipient are both legitimate. Internet access makes everything extremely easy to research. Anyone can gain knowledge, validate facts and sharpen senses with education by using electronic resources.

S
cams and scammers are becoming more popular and need to be reported whenever there is question. There are multiple ways scammers are active in the electronic world. Scams appear in many forms and are often attached to emails, chats, ads, maps, navigation tools, videos, photos, etc. Scammers are often professional at their scamming and therefore gain access to information easily.

A
ny and all suspicious or unusual activity in the electronic communication world should be questioned, noted and reported. Do not waste time or get involved when there may be a scam scenario. Do not hesitate to report to a scam hotline. Most hotlines have toll free access and accept complaints regarding scams. Research is your best defense.

Warnings of precarious scenarios and potential dangerous situations:

1. What if everyone who uses electronic devices was curious enough to *research scams or scammers by using an electronic search engine?*

2. What if an *email or messaging picture was pasted in an electronic search bar* to research: would it display good results?

3. What if an email or chat *message has broken language and poor grammar*: should it be electronically researched?

4. What if an electronic *message asks for any kinds of donations*: should it be researched in an electronic search bar for verification?

5. What if an electronic *message of any kind sounds too good to be true*: should it be electronically researched for validation?

6. What if an email or chat contains an abstract *hard luck story*: should it be electronically researched for confirmation?

7. What if *scammers are building email lists to collect personal information*: should everyone research how to secure personal information and electronic devices?

8. What if an email or chat *asks for personal information too soon*: should the message be researched immediately for authentication?

9. What if scams are designed to detour activity away from the sight so *scammers could gather personal data to use in a fraudulent event:* should it be researched?

10. What if *scam hotlines* could be posted everywhere so everyone could become more aware of scammers: would electronic usage be safer for everyone?

~About the author~

I often wonder why many authors use a pseudonym when publishing a book. Now, with such understandings, I also prefer to utilize an alias to represent me throughout the writing community's.

My family has often said in jest that I was like an old oak tree, so I feel it is an appropriate title because of description given to a Willow Oak.

A Willow Oak tree roots itself deep into the ground spreading its roots as extensions while above the ground extends its branches upward and outward in consistent directions producing entire coverings of delicate leaves. The core of a Willow Oak is a hard, heavy, solid wood that is used to build many buildings that represents the legacy of the tree.

At this time I claim the pen name *Willow Oakes* to honor my maternal heritage and to proceed with my own family legacy.

~ ©Willow Oakes ~